Women of
the 1960s

*For Michael, with my love and thanks for sharing the
ups and downs of life with me since 1964.*

Other Books by the Same Author:

A 1950s Housewife: Marriage and Homemaking in the 1950s.
A 1950s Mother: Bringing Up Baby in the 1950s.
The Real Mrs Beeton: The Story of Eliza Acton.
Suffolk: Murder and Crime.
Arsenic in the Dumplings: A Casebook of Suffolk Poisonings.
The Cretingham Murder.
Frances, Lady Nelson: The Life and Times of an Admirable Wife.
The House on the Hill: The Samford House of Industry, 1764-1930.
Tattingstone: A Village and its People.
Treason's Flame.
The Diary of a Suffolk Farmer's Wife: 1854-69.
The Story of Anne Candler.
1804 ... That was the Year ...
The Village School

Women of the 1960s

More Than Mini Skirts, Pills and Pop Music

Sheila Hardy

PEN & SWORD
HISTORY

First published in Great Britain in 2015 by
Pen & Sword History
an imprint of
Pen & Sword Books Ltd
47 Church Street
Barnsley
South Yorkshire
S70 2AS

Copyright © Sheila Hardy 2015

ISBN 978 1 47383 439 2

The right of Sheila Hardy to be identified as the Author of this Work
has been asserted by her in accordance with the Copyright, Designs
and Patents Act 1988.

A CIP catalogue record for this book is available from the British
Library

Printed and bound in the UK by CPT Group (UK) Ltd,

Pen & Sword Books Ltd incorporates the imprints of Pen & Sword
Archaeology, Atlas, Aviation, Battleground, Discovery, Family
History, History, Maritime, Military, Naval, Politics, Railways, Select,
Transport, True Crime, and Fiction, Frontline Books, Leo Cooper,
Praetorian Press, Seaforth Publishing and Wharncliffe.

For a complete list of Pen & Sword titles please contact
PEN & SWORD BOOKS LIMITED
47 Church Street, Barnsley, South Yorkshire, S70 2AS, England
E-mail: enquiries@pen-and-sword.co.uk
Website: www.pen-and-sword.co.uk

Contents

List of Illustrations

Leaving tradition behind, this was the very latest style for wedding dresses c. 1962.

This very detailed invoice for a wedding reception in 1969 shows how prices increased during the decade.

The invoice for the fashionable teak bedroom suite does not include the bed itself.

Lovely though the baby is, it is the Sixties' furnishings that are of interest. Note the patterned carpet, tiled fireplace and the very popular 'Gladiator' companion set as the fire-irons were called.

With this versatile ladder system, one could customise shelves and units to suit one's own needs and taste. They were very fashionable in the new open-plan living rooms.

The memorable freezing winter of 1963. This was the scene on 31 December 1962. Much more snow was to follow.

During the winter of 1963 a group of Suffolk students went on an Outward Bound course to Wales.

That precious driving licence that gave women their freedom.

The Morris Minor 1000 was probably the most popular car in the 1960s. Here we have R., who was encouraged to learn to drive as soon as she was old enough, in the school uniform she wore to take her test.

Those were the days, when petrol was around five shillings (25p) a gallon (approx. 4·5 litres). Five gallons almost filled the Austen Mini's tank.

A very determined-looking J.T. on her large scooter. Young women loved the freedom they gave.

An example of the small advertisements which appeared in women's magazines. These show that many women were still making not only their own clothes but household items too. The corsetry item catered for those large-waisted women who were unable to buy garments their size in the shops.

This shows the summer fashions that were available both in shops and by post (a forerunner of on-line shopping) in the Sixties.

Sixth-form girls out of uniform, ready for an evening at the theatre at Stratford-upon-Avon. It is likely they were all wearing the fashionable stiffened petticoats to make their skirts stand out.

Such was the interest in music in the Sixties that even the very young were playing records on the popular portable players. In this rather minimalist living room we see that television sets have grown in size since the 1950s.

In the summer term of 1961, a group of A-level students set off from Dorset in a bus with its lady driver to spend five days on a tour of Shakespeare country, including a visit to the newly-restored Coventry Cathedral and a Jane Austen day in Bath.

G. in her pushchair being wheeled ashore after the long voyage with other migrants to Australia in 1960.

How small this aircraft about to start on a long-haul flight from Nigeria to Heathrow seems compared to the aircraft of today.

An unusual Guinness advertisement in that it was aimed specifically at women and the benefits it could bring to their health. During the 1960s nursing mothers were often encouraged to drink stout but the advert suggests that all women could benefit from a Guinness.

Acknowledgements

Without the help of the following women (and those who chose anonymity) who shared their personal memories of life in the 1960s, this book would lack authenticity. To them all I give my heartfelt and most grateful thanks.

Mesdames Austin; Baggot; Baty; Bell; Best; Binns; Bixler; Bolton; Burnham; Bush; Clift; Cobley; Dicks; Donohue; Emery; Evans; Green; Hann; Harris; Hartley; Hatelie; Henderson; Hill; Horsburgh; Kahawatte; Kerswell; Kilworth; Ling; McGill; Marsh; Newbold; O'Halloran; Porte; Rees; Richardson; Rigby; Smith; Squirrell; Taylor; Thomas; M. and S. Troll; Todd; Turner; Wetherick; Woodman; and Drs Henman and Lewis.

And in loving memory of Margaret Postle and Dot Randall.

Special thanks too, to those who searched their family photograph albums: P. Atkins; G. Evans; D. Hann; J. McGill; R. Rigby; G. Squirrell; and C. Woodman. Other illustrations from the author's collection.

I am indebted to Susan Emery and Ursula Hardy for preserving the magazines from the 1960s they so generously allowed me to study: *Everywoman*, September 1964; *Woman and Home*, April 1969; *Family Circle*, March 1969; *Pins and Needles*, December 1968; and *Stitchcraft*, April 1969.

Valerie Clift and Sarah Hardy need a special mention for their patient and painstaking reading of the typescript.

Finally I acknowledge with my sincere thanks the kindness and generosity of David Abbot of Time Inc (UK); Nigel Penderleith, MD of Blue Max Banner Ltd; and The Global Team of DIAGEO.

Introduction: 'The Swinging Sixties'

The conversation at table turned to recollections of decades past and youthful indiscretions. Immediately, animated voices, mainly female, were raised as guests tried to relate their personal memories of that decade. One guest volunteered that living and working in the Far East, he had totally missed out on the 1960s. In the ensuing lull, his wife gently reminded him that between the years 1964 and 1968, they had met, married and bought their first house, only to leave it within eighteen months when he had secured his dream job and they had to locate to another part of the country where, a year later, their elder son was born. While he remembered accurately the day and the month of some of these events, somehow the years themselves were more elusive. To the amusement of the other diners their conversation was in danger of becoming a parody of that sad duet from the musical *Gigi*, 'Ah yes, I remember it well'! It became clear that for him the so-called Swinging Sixties meant The Beatles, and it was true that he was indeed living abroad when the Fab Four and their music made such an impact on the youth of the country. It would seem that hindsight and the media have imbued the decade of the 1960s with a rosy glow of carefree youth, pop music and miniskirts. Freedom and frivolity are the catchwords used to describe those days. For those who had not been born then, the mystique that now surrounds those years takes no account of the many serious issues both at home and in the wider world that gave deep concern at the time, some of which have either still to be resolved or have re-emerged to be with us today.

From that supper conversation it became clear that for the majority of those present, the 1960s had been passed as a decade in which they, to quote the words of one of the men, 'had been busy earning a living and making a home for the family'. However, it was one of the women who remarked that she had actually enjoyed that decade more than any other in her life, while another chimed in that for her it had been a very exciting time. It was these and similar remarks that sparked off the idea of finding out what life then had really been like for a wide cross section of women. With memories recalled after nearly fifty years, women, whose ages ranged from those who had still been at school in the Sixties to those who were more mature, gave very precise and sometimes incredibly intimate details of their lives. In written accounts some long-held secrets were revealed such as teenage pregnancies, the consequences of which highlighted parental attitudes to the situation based on the accepted social mores of the time. Far from freedom and frivolity, for the girls concerned it was either a hastily-arranged wedding or banishment to another part of the country until the resulting baby could be put up for adoption so that no one outside the immediate family need know of the disgrace the daughter had brought upon them. 'What will the neighbours say?' was a mantra which often dominated the attitude of many older parents just as much in the Sixties as it had done in the Fifties.

The post-war recovery of the country as a whole had brought an increase in prosperity for many which in turn fuelled a market for those with a disposable income. With many families no longer depending on the wages brought home by their children to supplement the family's weekly budget, working teenagers had money to spend as they wished. And for a large number this meant they were able to buy the records of their favourite singers, plaster their bedroom walls with posters of their pop idols, most of whom at that time were American, and even buy tickets for live performances. On an everyday basis, youth clubs now provided meeting places for them to dance or just listen to records, in turn encouraging young musicians to form their own groups. Youth groups which had in the past often been single sex, affiliated to a religious denomination and devoted to learning skills and working for the good of others, now became centres for pleasure, perhaps surprisingly, still run – and supervised – by the church. These mixed clubs, however, provided not just the opportunity to meet members of the opposite sex but for many they also cut across social barriers, perhaps for the first time. Previously, friends were made either at school, in the local neighbourhood or were the children of their parents' friends. Now, sometimes to their dismay, parents had no idea of the background of the friends of their son or daughter. This was particularly worrying for the fathers of girls and their heavy-handed attempt at control frequently led to family discord.

But what of those girls who left home? Greater educational opportunities meant that many more girls stayed on at school until they were eighteen to gain the qualifications that would take them to university, teacher training college or to a teaching hospital for nursing – or even medical – training. Suddenly it seemed the opportunities for women were endless: very few professions were not open to women who were prepared to fight for the right to enter them. These girls found freedom from home and parental control but most of them discovered that rules governing Halls of Residence, Nurses Home or Hostels for Young Women did not allow them the total freedom they might have hoped for. Doors were locked at 10.30, late passes a special concession not a right and men were allowed in rooms only under strict rules. In other words the establishment replaced their parents and a dressing down from the Warden or Matron could be far worse than anything Mum or Dad said. But these eighteen- or nineteen-year-old girls had to learn to take responsibility for themselves, not least having to learn how to do things mother had always done. They studied hard, played sports, enjoyed a social life and learned the hard way how to budget on their grant.

Sixties women as a whole were more assured than many of their predecessors; they wanted to have a career, be independent and to enjoy themselves. They were not fighting for equality – mostly they took that for granted. But they did want marriage and children too and thus they set the trend for the 21st-century women to have it all. However, before we look at what their lives were really like, it is necessary to go back into what led up to the so-called 'Swinging Sixties'.

In the olden days historical events were labelled as belonging to a particular century or centuries or a reign, for example the Middle Ages or Medieval Times, a period that covered several hundred years, or several individual reigns were lumped together as in the Tudors, Stuarts and Georgians. The two great queens of the past, Elizabeth I and Victoria, both have their own periods but after Victoria historical time spans seem to have become shorter. Who decided that we should start talking about the twentieth century in decades? Had life become so very fast-changing that we could differentiate one set of ten years from another? Or was it that it was easier for the Press to talk about certain events in a decade under a label such as 'The Depression' for the Thirties, which only covered a small part of all the other events of that era? The Press must bear some of the responsibility but can it also rest with some of the school history textbooks that were published from the 1950s? At a time when much in education was deemed to be out of date, history was probably top of the list. Those who studied the subject during the Second World War and the immediate post-war years will testify to the rather dry academic approach adopted in most of their textbooks, with an emphasis on Britain's past glories in battles and its imperial expansion. The school syllabus decreed the teaching of the facts of the Agrarian and Industrial

Revolutions, the Corn Laws, the Chartist Movement and the growth of Trades Unions alongside the political influence of Castlereagh, Canning, Peel and other luminaries. The problem was that often these subjects were dealt with in isolation and thus seemed to have no relevance at all to the life of the average pupil. The hardest question any history teacher ever has to answer is 'what's the purpose of learning history?'.

The new era of educationalists set out to make history relevant – and exciting! The idea was that the pupil should become involved, and, should the subject be child labour, for example, feel empathy with those who were involved at the time. Instead of going back to the Victorian reformers who had conducted first hand investigations and written vivid accounts of their findings, some of the books produced at this time were written a bit like comic books. Brightly-coloured pictures with snippets of information conveyed in speech bubbles told a story that was intended to make the reader feel that they too were sent down the mines or worked long hours in a dangerous factory. Appealing though this approach might be, the authors rarely filled in the essential background, why it happened the way it did. It could be argued that where the old texts had been conservative (with a small 'c') in their approach, these modern books, with the emphasis on the grinding down of the poor at the hands of the hard-hearted money-grabbing rich, had their own political message to convey. We need to be wary of this empathetic approach. It makes for good emotional television viewing when those researching their family background tearfully express their shocked horror on discovering that a Victorian antecedent had ended up in the workhouse. Instead of looking at the situation from the comfort of their 21st-century life, they should stop to consider what would have been the reality of the alternative and give thanks that there was a system in place that gave a family a roof over their heads, warm clothing, three meals a day and education for the children. Was that not better than being homeless, having to rely on begging – or worse? It is difficult to arrive at a balanced view of the subject, but we should try.

There is another problem when discussing what life was like in a certain decade. No one is naïve enough to believe as Big Ben strikes midnight on 31 December in the year that ends a decade, that overnight everything is going to change. Even momentous changes such as a declaration of war or the change from imperial weights to metric take time to percolate through the system. So how can we talk about life in one decade being so very different from the one before it or the one that will come after? And just for the record, when exactly did the Sixties, for example, start? Was 1960 the end of the Fifties or the beginning of the Sixties? Some may remember the question being asked as the Millennium approached; were we to celebrate as the year 2000 dawned or wait until 2001? Did it really matter, cynics replied. All of which means that before we look at the Sixties, we need to have some idea of what was going on during the latter years of the Fifties so that we can see what did change and why.

By the end of the Fifties, Britain was beginning to recover from post-war austerity. Industry was getting into full swing throughout the country, producing both essential and luxury goods for the home market. Factories which had been turned over to making munitions could now concentrate on manufacturing electrical goods; cars and lorries; aeroplanes, now for business and foreign trade as well as the fast-growing holiday travel market rather than for fighting; and new industries like the Atomic Energy Authority were using nuclear power to generate electricity to replace the country's dwindling coal supplies. Both old and new industries provided plenty of jobs, which was good news for the workforce – except that many of those workers needed somewhere to live. After the war the building industry had been faced with the enormous task of trying to replace all the houses destroyed during the bombing while at the same time adding new homes to satisfy the needs of the rising numbers of married couples. The biggest problem the industry faced initially was the acute shortage of essential materials, which meant that the government imposed restrictions on the size of privately-built houses. There are still areas where a box-like bungalow with no more room than was available in the old late Victorian two-up two-down terraced house sits in the middle of a plot of land that could accommodate four semis complete with garages. Since local councils were expected to provide housing for those in need, they were given permission to build new estates, often on agricultural land on the outskirts of towns and as the situation eased whole new towns were created which allowed modern planners to try to get rid of all the mistakes of the past.

But none of this happened overnight. Even in the mid-1960s few young couples moved into their own house on marriage. Most either started living with one or other set of parents or rented a living room and bedroom in someone else's home as they would have done in the Fifties. At that time when they had worked their way 'up the housing ladder', which as in the 1950s meant that they had gained the necessary points either by having an essential job – nurse, midwife, fireman, policeman or teacher, or that they had had a second child: even then, in those areas where the shortage was most acute, initially this gave them only a half-share in a new house until the situation eased.

Probably one of the biggest changes at this time was the change in attitude to home ownership. Some people are surprised to find that 'every Englishman's castle', that is, his home, was not usually owned by him. Historically, land and often the houses built upon it belonged to a very small portion of the population. Great landed estates were handed down through generations and the people who worked the land had their farmhouses and cottages provided for them and they paid rent to the landowner. Even in London most of the large, fashionable houses were owned by a few individuals who made their income by renting them to others perhaps for a season or on a long lease. With industrialisation came the need to have a workforce on tap, so rented housing was built for those who flocked to different parts of the country seeking work. Even the more affluent middle class, who moved out to the leafy suburbs to a large well-built villa with a garden, still rented from the entrepreneurs who had discovered that owning houses brought them a steady income.

After the First World War it had become the duty of the local city, town and district councils to provide decent, affordable homes for their area and so the term 'council house' was born. Usually built to a high standard, the homes were also provided with large gardens so that the occupants could help themselves financially by growing their own vegetables. The council also maintained the houses, doing necessary roof repairs for example and decorating the exterior at regular intervals. Admittedly, this meant the occupants had no choice as to the colour of the front door or window frames, everyone had the same. Then in the late Thirties came small local builders who began to buy up land and speculatively build semi-detached houses, which they offered for sale and so began the whole process of ordinary people saving for a deposit and then approaching a building society for a mortgage. Then came the war but by the 1960s, people were again responding to the idea of having a brand new house that they would actually own, even if it was twenty-five years later.

Home ownership was not the only aspect of life that was changing; barriers would be broken down between the classes and between the relative status of men and women; educational opportunities would be open to all regardless of income. With the growth in consumerism that resulted from high employment, a feeling was propagated that what had been considered luxury goods should be available to all, not just those we had considered to be our social superiors. But the biggest change came in the attitudes of young people in this country who came under the influence of the American lifestyle brought to them through the medium of films, television, magazines and music. Young Britons were being fed images which depicted what was assumed to be the everyday life of their young American counterparts; in high school and colleges; riding motorcycles or driving huge open-top cars; going to dances and drive-in movies; eating exciting-looking fast food from takeaways, sipping Coca-Cola or eating ice-cream sundaes in a cafeteria furnished with bright red Formica tables while the latest singer's music played on the jukebox in the background. Parallel with this was the change that had been wrought slowly into schools since the mid-Fifties with the introduction of the comprehensive secondary education system. In the name of true social equality, it was decided that the much maligned Eleven-Plus examination which decided if a child should attend a grammar school or a secondary modern should be abolished and all children, regardless of academic ability, would, as in the United States, be educated together in a large purpose-built school in their neighbourhood. Naturally, this could not happen immediately but bit-by-bit, existing schools were either merged with another locally – often resulting in a split campus (a word borrowed from America) or closed down completely. Generally speaking co-education before the 1960s had been rare; where it did exist it was more likely to have been the result of economy rather than ideology. The new system brought with it problems such as uniform which had always been a bone of contention, dismissed as being too expensive for the average family to afford. Many teachers emerging from training college had been influenced by zealous lecturers who regarded the whole attitude to education as being too rigid and formal, so discipline became more relaxed and stories circulated of casually-dressed teachers who sat on the desk, demanded to be called by their first name and did not believe it was their place to set an example to pupils or try to keep them in order. Thus it was hardly surprising that parents found their adolescents were no longer as willing to listen to their parents as they had been. But as we shall find out, the so-called Swinging Sixties were not at all as we have been led to believe.

It is often said today that 21st-century woman tries to have it all – career, husband, family and all the accessories that make for a comfortable life. Many do, but with all generalisations, there are a great many more for whom life is a real struggle. However, we must remember that these young women are just starting out on their life path. If one can draw any conclusions from the lives of the now ageing 1960s women, it would be this, that in many ways, they have managed to have it all.

All the contributors, whatever their initial backgrounds, have gone on to take all the opportunities that came their way to achieve happy, useful and fulfilling lives. Those who married young, perhaps at the outset of their careers, often gave up work to become full-time mothers, some having more than the standard two point four children, often very closely together. Many, indeed most, struggled financially, often undertaking 'piecework' when the children were in bed to help the family income. Others studied to improve their qualifications while others took time to reassess what their future career should be, for all of them had assumed that they would resume work once the children were of school age. For example, the bright young journalist decided to train as a nurse, then not satisfied with that went on to become a health visitor where her forte lay, later becoming a much sought-after lecturer in this field. Some went into teaching, which they found to be a more satisfying career than, for example, working in isolation in a science laboratory, while others were able to satisfy an ambition to start their own business.

Among those who remained unmarried were the women who were prepared to seize the opportunity to travel and live abroad, taking posts in the Foreign Office, education, the medical profession and scientific research projects around the world. Life as a long-serving member of one of the armed Services provided opportunities that once would have been unthinkable for a woman. Others continued their careers at home at the same time assuming responsibility for elderly parents. These women were also the much-loved aunts and godmothers who indulged and gave good advice to young nieces, nephews and godchildren – the unpaid babysitters who were never too busy to listen to the worries and woes of others.

The 1960s women were the ones who got together to start playgroups and informal baby-sitting services; who helped with Sunday Schools, Brownies and Cubs, ran dancing classes, the Junior Red Cross Cadets, Guides and sports teams. In fact, whenever a volunteer was required, they answered the call, not just because their child might be involved but also because someone had to do these things. These were the women who gained the confidence to become active in the their Trades Union at work; who felt strongly enough about the affairs of their local area to stand for election to their local parish or town council. From there it was on to district or county level and for the really keen, the next step might be Parliament itself. Age was no barrier for

1960s women. The young Shirley Caitlin (later to become Williams) was only twenty-four when she contested the seat for Harwich in 1954 and after another abortive attempt she won Hitchin for Labour in 1964 – still only in her early thirties.

As their family needs changed and they had more time, they were likely to throw themselves into more voluntary work for charities; social concerns like the Citizens' Advice Bureau and the Samaritans, perhaps becoming Justices of the Peace. As each decade passed so there were more and more opportunities for the 1960s' women to play a major role. Retirement from paid employment simply gave them more time to take up new causes to add to those they already had, but it also brought on the new challenge of reverting back to childcare. In many cases, to give 21st-century woman the chance to achieve all she wants, grandmothers throughout the country are helping relieve the heavy burden of the cost of professional childcare by looking after their grandchildren several days a week. The women of the 1960s have achieved it all. They are not left feeling redundant; they still have a major role to play influencing the lives of the next generation.

Looking back, the 1960s seemed to be full of endless possibilities; engineering had produced smart new cars; aeroplanes were becoming much bigger and capable of much longer journeys without having to stop to refuel; designers were creating new and exciting concepts for buildings as well as furniture; the whole world was being brought into our living rooms via television; outer space had been conquered and there was even the prospect – actually achieved in 1969 – of men walking on the moon. Women accepted and made use of all the innovations that came their way. Had you told them that the day would come when they would walk around with a telephone no bigger than the powder compact in their handbag and that they would not only be able to talk to but also see their grandchildren on the other side of the world, they would have laughed in disbelief. They would have said that that was as likely as the wild idea that traffic congestion would be relieved by us all having individual jet-packs which would allow us to fly above street level.

Disbelief, because for the majority of the population at that time the only access they had to a telephone was the heavy black instrument found in the ubiquitous red kiosks placed in convenient places all over the country. It was all very well the GPO, who was responsible for the telephone service, building the innovative Post Office Tower, which dominated the London skyline when it opened in 1965. Its famous revolving restaurant at the top might afford diners with the most spectacular views but throughout the country many thousands of people were on waiting lists to have a telephone installed in their homes. That year may have celebrated the installation of the ten millionth telephone – in Hampstead as it happened – but in a village just outside Canterbury S.M. was still waiting to be linked up to her local exchange. She was one of the lucky ones, the wait was only a few months, and so she was amazed when on moving to Harwich in 1968, that although her husband's job was classified as priority for a telephone, there was still a wait before they were eventually allocated a shared party line.

It was not just a shortage of telephones: there were still homes in many parts of the country which lacked essential services like an electricity supply, mains water and sewage disposal, proper kitchens, bathrooms and lavatories, particularly in rural areas. There might be some excuse in really remote areas where houses, usually farms, were miles from their neighbours, but even villages on the edge of big towns were lacking in services that townspeople took for granted. All of which emphasises that progress for some was very slow and that the 1960s were not necessarily as bright and cheerful as legend would have us believe.

Chapter One

Life after School

In the 1960s all pupils could legally leave school when they reached fifteen and they did not have to wait until the end of the school year in July, they could, if they wished, go in December. In some ways this was a good thing as it meant that a general exodus from the schools in the summer did not flood the labour market. Those girls who attended secondary modern schools, that is, the majority of the female population, were more likely to leave at the earliest opportunity. Girls who were at grammar schools were expected to stay until they were sixteen, or had completed the five years of education which culminated in the taking of the GCE O level examinations. Only in extraordinary circumstances were girls allowed to go before that. In most cases the 'circumstances' meant that the girls concerned were pregnant – or at least that was the rumour which usually did the rounds.

Public examinations were not offered to the majority of girls, so most of them entered the workplace without any paper qualifications. Some schools did offer a commercial course which taught shorthand, typing and book-keeping, so successful students with a certificate of competency issued by the Royal Society of Arts (RSA) were able to present themselves for jobs in offices. Finding work at that time seemed relatively easy as some of these women revealed.

I left school in 1964 aged 15 and went straight to work in an electronics factory that did small assembly work, but being the newcomer my jobs included helping the tea-lady take the tea round to all the other workers, sweeping the factory floor and numerous other odd jobs – including once being sent to the stores department for a long weight! I felt very grown up and had to pay my way in the world. I think my pay was £1.10s a week, the pound of which was given to my Mum for my keep.

Ten shillings (50p) would have seemed quite a generous sum for J. until she realised she had to buy her clothes, and all the other items that a girl needed, as well as trying to save some of it. The question of parents expecting their working children to contribute to the housekeeping expenses was a vexed one. It was a perennial on the Problem Page of most women's magazines; not so much should the young pay towards their keep but rather how much should parents expect them to pay? Many parents thought they should ration a young wage-earner's pocket money. The gentle but ambiguous advice was that while it all depended on circumstances, the Agony Aunts felt that the young should learn to handle money for themselves and so become thrifty. In many cases what actually happened was that if it were not needed for the family, the mother would take a portion of the wages and secretly put it into a savings account ready for when the daughter married.

P. also left her secondary modern at fifteen without any qualifications. She worked for three years as a trainee window-dresser in a clothes shop. That sounded both creative and the first steps to a proper career but she was in her own words 'only a glorified junior sales assistant'. When the shop closed down she worked in the gown department of a local department store which she thought sounded very grand – as the rest of the assistants like to think they were! After a year there, she left to get married.

J. and P. both married young, at eighteen and nineteen respectively, and neither appeared to have had any real ambition as far as a career was concerned. Other girls did, but unfortunately for them, it was their parents who decided what path they should follow. M.O. was a very shy child who had not enjoyed her time at school. So it was not surprising, bearing in mind the problems they had had with her own schooling, that her parents were taken aback when she suddenly announced at the beginning of her final year that she wanted to be a teacher. Not only did they think she was totally unsuitable, there was the economic consideration that this would mean: prolonging her education in order to gain the required examinations necessary for entry to teacher training college in addition to the further two years before she was qualified. So her parents agreed it was out of the question and settled on the sensible solution of many parents at that time, insisting she took advantage of the commercial class that was available in her final year at school. A girl could not go wrong if she had shorthand and typing qualifications. So M.O. found herself at fifteen in her first employment as a junior clerk, not in a small cosy office but in the design department of one of the larger factories in her home town that made corsetry and ladies' underwear. After a week or so when M.O.'s boss discovered she could take shorthand, he began dictating letters for her to type up. This shy young girl nearly died from embarrassment when a man began talking about 'directoire' knickers and other female undergarments of which she knew little. Fortunately she did not have to endure the situation for long. The local Employment Exchange, following up its placement of school leavers, sent her a note asking if she was happy in her work: if not, then there were several other jobs available that might suit her. She called at the Labour Exchange after work and was given an appointment for Saturday morning for another job. She was too shy to ask for time off during working hours, hence the Saturday arrangement. She got that job. Others followed until five years later she was the private secretary to a solicitor. At which point, she too got married.

In contrast fifteen-year-old S. left school knowing exactly what she wanted to do, but she was, alas, too young. She left school on a Friday and the following Monday started work as a nanny (untrained) to the three children of her local doctor, a job she held for the next eighteen months, spending her evenings studying and attending evening classes in order to get the qualifications needed to start training to be a nurse.

I then became a nursing cadet at the local hospital. This was really the lowest rank and you were not allowed to forget it! In the dining room you were not allowed to sit at a table with staff above your rank unless invited to do so. That rule remained through the whole of my training. Uniforms had to be a certain length off the floor and no jewellery at all was permitted with the exception of a wedding ring. All staff had to live in the Nurses' Home while training and there were very strict rules. Everyone had to be in by 10.30 p.m. unless you had seen Matron for a late night pass. This was not an easy task, as she wanted to know where you were going and who you were going with! So unless you could bribe the nurse whose bedroom window was on the fire escape to let you in, you had to comply. No males were allowed in the Home at all.

Eleven days after S. started her training she met her future husband and over the next six years they met two or three times a week, one or the other travelling the twenty-five miles that parted them, he borrowing his older sister's car or S. spending 3s 6d on a return train ticket. Of their six-year courtship S. writes: 'As fitted the time, we were good, no sex, no drugs, no rock and roll – but we did go to the jazz club, now and then!'

Girls who left the grammar schools at sixteen with five or more O levels to their credit were usually better equipped to find a wider choice of occupation. A whole new world was opening up for those with good grades in maths and the sciences. Not only was their work likely to be interesting, even stimulating, but they could also earn higher wages. A grammar-school teacher with a degree and five years' experience was somewhat taken aback when, in 1960, she discovered that one of her O-level students had found a job at ITV with a salary that was equal to her own! That, of course, was not the case for most sixteen-year-olds.

T. wrote:

I left the High School at 16 in 1963. I got a job straight away. Looking back, it seemed that getting a job was easy. I worked in a quality control laboratory in a Maltings in Bury St Edmunds. This meant that every morning my father gave me a lift to Lavenham where I caught a bus to Bury. I got to Bury about an hour before I was due to start work so usually I went to a coffee bar before setting off to walk the mile to work. My starting wage was £5 a week, which I received in a pay packet every Friday. I had 'dinner' every day in the staff canteen. In the evening I got the bus back to Lavenham and then caught another to my home.

J.M. also attended the High School in a busy Suffolk market town. She had her sights set on going to do a secretarial course at Colchester Technical College, but because the High School had a secretarial course of its own, her parents decided she should stay on another year and do that. However, when she did leave school she was able to join the second year of a two-year course at the Technical College in 1966.

I remember it being so different from school – feeling so 'grown-up'. For a start, there were boys and I'd come from an all-girls school! But we were expected to get on with our work and be self-motivated which was also different from before. I loved my year at the Tech, made lots of friends; had lots of fun. I worked hard and ended up with really good qualifications, both secretarial and adding two more GCEs. My first job was in the Admin Dept at Essex University in Colchester. I was earning £9 a week. A year or so later I applied and got the job as a secretary to the Managing Director of a Petroleum company in my hometown. I was now earning £11 a week and no longer had to travel.

It is interesting to note how the salaries were rising during the course of the latter part of the Sixties. The previous account mentions Essex University, one of the new modern seats of learning which came into being during that period to meet the need for more higher education places. The design of the

Essex campus was startling; the stark concrete inward-looking skyscrapers have been called 'Brutalist' but in the words of the local inhabitants it was 'modern' – the word being uttered with a certain curl of lip!

The number of girls going on to further education rose sharply in the 1960s. This was partly due to a change in the attitude of some parents who realised that it was worthwhile educating their daughters for a career even if they would probably get married and start a family. After all, there were so many more opportunities now for a girl to earn a good living, which should give her a chance to save towards the house she and her husband would eventually buy. And should the daughter not get married, they argued, then a career would provide her with a more-than-adequate standard of living. Furthermore, there was a more general acceptance of the idea put forward years before by missionaries working in foreign countries, that if you educated a woman there was a strong chance that you would be teaching a future generation. Economically, too, many families were no longer dependent on their children going out to work as soon as possible to help with the family finances, so they could afford to help towards their daughter's keep. And of course, since the late 1940s, those students who had won university places were awarded a grant by their local Education Authority, which paid their tuition fees and contributed towards their accommodation and general living costs. How much this grant amounted to depended to some extent on parental income, which in effect meant that students from poorer backgrounds were no longer barred from a higher education through lack of funds. Unfortunately it also depended on how many students in their area were seeking grants, which led to an unfair distribution of funding. The term 'postcode lottery' was unknown then since postcodes hadn't been invented, but the principle was the same – the more populated towns and cities had to eke out their pot of money to more students, while the few who came from the larger, mainly rural counties each received sometimes twice as much. In an area where requests for grants were high, preference seems to have been given to boys rather than girls.

Girls staying on at school until eighteen saw that their friends who had gone into work were now able to buy themselves the clothes they wanted, while the Sixth Former was still dependent on her parents to provide her needs. The more affluent ones could afford to do this and frequently gave the girl a monthly allowance as well to cover all the extras she might need. However, many of those staying on came from homes where in times past parents would have expected that by sixteen their daughter would be almost independent or even contributing to the family's housekeeping expenses. The answer here was for the girl to find a part-time job at weekends and during the school holidays. The availability of such employment depended very much on where one lived. Those in seaside resorts easily found work in hotels, boarding houses and cafes during the peak of the summer season, but were limited for the rest of the year; those in towns and cities had a much wider choice and W.'s Saturday job must have been the envy of many. Having cut her teeth, as it were, in the local greengrocer's where she enjoyed meeting the customers, selecting and wrapping fruit and vegetables and then adding up the prices in her head, she moved on to the dizzy heights of Woolworths:

I worked on the biscuit and sweet counter; a treasure trove. The starched white cotton overalls varied in size and luck dictated whether we got one that fitted. The headbands had the red Woolworth logo embroidered on the front. The trick was to clip it as far back on the hair as the management would allow. The uniforms were hateful to a teenager interested in fashion, but the wages were good and we had a surprisingly tasty midday meal cooked for us in a tiny alcove kitchen, which we ate around a domestic-sized table in the cramped dining room. Because we were not allowed to appear not to be occupied at any given moment, we had to arrange and rearrange the counter tops when there were no customers to serve. The counters were mahogany, huge and hollow. We made up bags of cashew nuts, hot from the roasted nut machine and disappeared under the counter to eat our unaffordable luxury amongst the biscuit tins, undetected.

W.'s next foray into part-time work is included here for several reasons as it touches on a number of aspects of life in the middle of the decade, but mainly because her descriptions are so vivid that it seemed wrong to attempt to paraphrase them.

The restaurant was small and stood at the end of the 1930s parade of shops. To mask the underlying seediness of the establishment each table had a candle on the paper cloth and at night these were lit. The diners sat in an intimate gloom served by the inexperienced waitress who wore a green check artist's smock with a floppy bow at the neck. Sometime in the past an unknown waitress had refused to wear the beret which completed this costume. Under this smock I usually wore a lined grey woollen flannel dress (probably made from a *Vogue* pattern) with a narrow black patent plastic belt, thick Black Watch tartan stockings. Black patent shoes with a little side strap and bow and kitten heels, which gathered collars of rotten lino by the end of the evening, completed the outfit. Away from the restaurant I added an emerald green Orlon or Courtelle (fine wool) cardigan. It was important to be as fashionable as possible at all times even though the smell of frying clung to the dress for days.

The menu never differed but I can only remember prawn cocktail, fried egg and chips, sausage and mash, mushroom omelette, spaghetti Bolognese, rice and green peppers, green salad and trout. I had to fish the frozen corpse from the bottom of a large chest freezer on demand. It was served grilled. My thick shoulder-length dark hair must have been an issue because an irritated customer sent back his empty plate with a message on the paper napkin telling me to get my hair cut. This may or may not be the guy who roasted his personal caterpillar over the candle flame!

Although W's account shows that some of the best comedy sketches from the past were not far from the truth, working in the restaurant left its mark on her life in that it was the chef's suggestion that she should go to art school (something she thought her parents would never countenance), and meeting two of the students whose paintings were displayed on the walls and offered for sale, that finally took root and led to her going to study at art college close to home and her subsequent career as a designer in advertising.

Most 1960s girls, however, have confided that they could not wait to get away from home. Some thought that their parents still exercised too much control over their lives once they had left school and started work. They longed to be independent yet, as we have seen from the earlier examples; some only escaped home life by getting married. The girls who did make the break with home were those who opted to study at university, technical colleges, teacher training colleges, in hospitals and medical schools or one of the prestigious secretarial colleges in London. And what a shock this breakaway was for many of them. To start with they often found themselves living in a different part of the country and working in an establishment that they had probably visited only once for their interview. And however much they had pored over the glossy brochure, it would not have prepared them for what lay in store when they started on their course.

How many of them while living at home had really given much thought to just how much they took for granted. Meals provided regularly, a bed to sleep in, sheets and towels changed and laundered, often their clothes also washed and ironed – and put away for them ... the list was endless, as no doubt their mothers frequently reminded them. Most prospective students expected that accommodation would be provided for them and a list would have been sent them telling how many pairs of single sheets and towels they needed to bring. When R. applied to Birmingham University, a couple of long train journeys from her home, she also applied for residence in the Women's Hall of Residence. What she had not realised was that while there were two large halls for men, there was only a single, much smaller one for women, and she had been allocated digs by the Lodgings Warden in a small private house. The sense of isolation this brought added to her homesickness. Eventually she was able to overcome both by getting a place in a hostel in the city run by The Girls' Friendly Society where she shared a very basic dormitory like room with two other girls. R. described the hostel as being not dissimilar to the one in Muriel Spark's *The Girls of Slender Means*, a novel that is an excellent evocation of the period. Living there was cheaper than the Hall of Residence, meals could be ordered in advance and guests could also be booked in for an evening meal. It was also possible to order bread and milk from the cook to use in their rooms, which were equipped with a gas ring as well as a gas fire. As long as the gas meter was fed with one shilling coins it was possible to make toast in front of the fire or boil a kettle or saucepan on the ring. The fire was essential in winter as there was no central heating in the building. There was still gas lighting on the landings. Old-fashioned though the building might be, the rules that governed the hostel seemed reasonable and were not as strictly enforced as those in the university halls, training colleges or nurses' homes.

The girls who found themselves living in one of these often complained that in many respects they felt they had exchanged their day school for a boarding one. Regularity at meals was insisted upon– no skipping them without special permission; in some establishments students were expected to be correctly dressed in the evening for dinner where the meal was served formally. Students were expected to be in by 10.30 p.m. at which time doors were locked. Late passes were given only by special request, which meant explaining why it was needed. The answer 'out' to the question 'where are you going?' may have worked with one's parents but certainly would not have satisfied the Warden or Matron. But the rule which amused female student more than any other was that regarding men in their rooms. While it was perfectly acceptable to invite a fellow student (male) into your room during the morning or afternoon, in the evening this was permissible only if one's roommate was also present and the young man had to leave by 10 o'clock. By the 1960s it is doubtful if there were many halls where beds had to be pushed into the corridor if a male entered a girl's room, as had once been the case, but most queried what it was that turned a male into a ravening beast after 6 p.m.

Rules, of course, did not just apply to living accommodation. Many of those coming straight from school were surprised to find that lectures took up most of the day and that they were expected to sign-in to each lecture. Some establishments threatened the student they would lose their grant if they skipped lectures. J.T. is a good example of a forward thinking female of the Sixties. She came from the sixth form of a small girls' grammar school that was used to its pupils going to university to read normal subjects such as English, History, Geography, French, German, Latin, Maths and Biology, that is most of the subjects which would equip them to become teachers. J.T. didn't want to do any of these; she wanted to do Industrial Chemistry.

> I felt that the school regarded that as something inferior and rather unpleasant! Also a College of Advanced Technology (to which I had applied) was a bit of a let-down to them. I think that they would have been much happier if I had done Ancient Greek at Oxford!! However, I knew better. This was the 1960s and technology was the future.

J.T.'s chosen route was different to anything the school had known. She had been accepted on a degree course in 1962 at the Northampton College of Advanced Technology situated in London, being named not after the town but after the Marquis of Northampton who gave the land including the London square which also bore his name. Two years later it became the City University as a result of the recommendations of the Robins Committee which had caused a big increase in demand for science places. Unlike the usual degree course of three years split into three ten-week terms per year, J.T.'s was a four-year sandwich course with six months spent at the University and the other half-year of each year spent working in an industrial laboratory. This was very intensive as it meant that three years' study had to be crammed into four six-monthly sessions with very little time left for holidays. In choosing to study what was an accepted male subject, J.T. found herself the only girl in her department – and one of only a handful in the entire university population, which was a bit daunting coming as she had from an all-girls school. She was very homesick in her first term and was reluctant to return after the Christmas break. But she persevered, accepting the fact that she would have to make friends who were boys, so she quickly learnt the words of the rugby songs and joined in the various rags and other male escapades in what she describes now as 'generally behaving in an idiotic but harmless fashion'.

Until the Hall of Residence opened in 1964, J.T. found accommodation in her first year in YWCA hostels very similar to the one described by R. Then in her second year, she must have felt she was at last leading an independent life when she moved into a one-bedroom flat on the west side of Regent's Park with an old school friend who was studying at Holborn College of Law, Language and Commerce. They shared the rent of seven guineas (£7.7s.0d) for accommodation which today would probably be condemned. It had an exploding gas geyser over the bath, which frightened them every time they used it. The only lavatory was shared with the other flats and was upstairs on the middle landing. After they moved in they received a polite note from the elderly lady on that landing asking them not to flush at night as it woke her up! Just round the corner from J.T.'s flat was the one occupied by Christine Keeler, who became famous for her part in the Profumo scandal. J.T. and her flatmate would often see her in the local butcher's but what really fascinated them was the large number of empty milk bottles always to be found on her doorstep. The girls wondered if this was some kind of code for her lovers.

When the University Hall of Residence finally opened, J.T. moved in. So very different to the older type of Hall, this was a seventeen floor, concrete block beside a huge hole in the ground that was noisily growing into the Barbican. The seventh floor was allotted to the women; all the rest was occupied by men.

> On Friday nights we aimed to stay up all night. We congregated in the 17th floor TV room, played poker until the early hours and then went out for a wander round the deserted streets of the City stopping for a fried egg roll in an all-night Fleet Street café and dropping into St Paul's Cathedral to hear the organist doing his early morning practising. We got back to Hall and queued for an early breakfast. No drink, no drugs.

What would those senior academic ladies who were wardens of women's halls around the country have made of that? But it shows how fast some parts of Sixties' life was moving.

While London was a magnet for lots of young women either studying or working, those who were taking degrees in languages at universities around the country had to spend six months of their course in the country of their main subject, so off they went to live in one or other of the European countries. But others ventured further afield. Long before backpacking to Australia or round the world became 'the in-thing' to do in the 'gap year' which many recent students have regarded as essential between leaving school and starting university, some Sixties students took part in the Voluntary Service Overseas scheme. Started initially for male students in 1958, when D. applied in 1963 it was open to women too. A young woman of very strong religious faith she had already made up her mind she wanted to teach and the prospect of going to do so in Africa spurred her on through the application and acceptance period. She was the first person from her school to be taken on and as she said 'quite suddenly found myself worthy of the headmaster's notice and congratulations. Not being a likely candidate for Oxbridge, he had thought me beneath his regard before.'

As the only child of loving parents, it must have been a wrench for all of them when the time came for her to depart. She knew she was to work for the World Affiliated YWCA in Bulawayo, Southern Rhodesia now Zimbabwe. But first she had to get there and for the average girl, particularly one who had never flown before this must have seemed daunting. Planes at that time rarely did a long haul flight non-stop, so for her it was stops at Rome, in the Sudan, Dar-es-Salaam, Nairobi, and Salisbury.

> We [she and another volunteer] were given a small flat, rent paid, in a mixed race area of the city and each day travelled into the African township of Mpopoma where under the loving and watchful eye of Eleanor Kumolo, we ran a YWCA centre. Not the more familiar hostel, instead we ran youth groups, literacy classes and went out into the bush to work with teenagers on a mission station; we organised social groups for nurses and made friends with African people from all walks of life; chiefs, MPs, doctors, illiterate Mums and beautiful children all of whom, it seemed, could sing like angels. On one occasion a group of us were invited with Mama Kumolo to a wedding. It had already been going for a week when they got there!

The whole experience made a tremendous impact on D.'s attitude to life. Not least she had to learn how to live on £10 a month with an allowance of £4 for pocket money. As a safeguard, all the Volunteers had to take £15 out with them from England in case of emergencies. That seems a laughable sum now but at that time the Government imposed restrictions on the amount of currency, including travellers' cheques, which UK residents were allowed to take out of the country.

As T. remarked earlier, jobs were plentiful in the 1960s, so that all the women who had gone on to higher education were not only able to find positions in the areas they wanted, often they were able to pick and choose between offers. However, there were still some employers who were reluctant to employ either newly-married women or those who girls who turned up for an interview wearing an engagement ring. Dr A. gives an example of the sexism she encountered first in the 1950s.

I had hoped to attend Durham University Medical School in Newcastle-upon-Tyne because my father qualified there. At my interview I was told that ninety percent of the places were for men and ten percent for women, of which one place was reserved for an overseas lady. I managed to get a place in the Dental School but was told I could not change to Medicine in my second year as I had hoped.

In Dublin I took an entrance exam. We were allocated a number so the examiners did not know if you were male, female, black, white or khaki! We had some ex-service people in my year, often old enough to be our fathers, so it gave a settled air. During Clinical work some lecturers tried to belittle the female students and often reduced them to tears. During the midwifery training we had to attend ten births in the hospital, then it was out into the district with the nurses showing you how to turn a home into a delivery room, then you were with a senior student and finally taking other students out with you. The patients were amazed to see the male students taking instructions from me – and for me to drive the ambulance.

After completing her training and becoming a Junior House Officer in a hospital in her a native Cumbria, Dr A. became caught up in the very severe influenza epidemic of 1957. She was sent to assist in a practice in the mining town of Millom where the senior GP had suffered a coronary. The only other woman doctor in the practice was married to the local police inspector and was supposed to work only part time but because of the senior's illness she had been working full time, flat out. Dr A noted that in those days there were men who refused to be treated by a woman but during the time she and the other doctor were running the practice no one left or refused treatment. She admits that since her father had previously had a practice in the town, the fact that she was known to some of the population may have helped. At the beginning of the Sixties she became a junior partner and started on her long career. She added two examples of the sexist treatment she received. One of the appointments that came with the practice was that of Doctor of Mines and Factories. It was not long before she received a letter rescinding the office with regard to the Mines as the miners said they did not like women in the mines. Actually, this was not quite the blow to her self-esteem, as it might have been because a month after she received the letter, the iron-ore mine closed. More amusing, but nonetheless a sexist rebuff, came when in her capacity as Factories Doctor she received an invitation to a dinner in Carlisle. She noted the words 'no lady guests' on the invitation, so was forced to confess that 'I was a female of the species'. It would have been a strong woman indeed who would have brazened it out and turned up but one suspects that on this occasion Dr A.'s good manners overrode any desire to make a stand for equality.

Two-thirds of the way through the decade, W. was about to leave art college and seek employment somewhere she could use her flair for design. After toting her portfolio of work around London, it was through answering an advertisement that she got a job in the publications department of Ilford Films which she enjoyed and paid £13 a week but involved a deadly commute from her home in north London. However, four months later she received another offer from a large City company to work in their design studio. Not only was this a big step up it brought an additional £5 increase in salary. However, between the time of the interview and her starting work at the studio W. had got engaged. S., the woman she was to work for, was shocked and upset when she turned up wearing her engagement ring and vowed that she would not have employed her had she known. However, she established not only a happy working relationship, but also a strong friendship with S. and her husband that W. was sorry to leave when she did eventually marry. With hindsight, W. recognises that she encountered examples of sexism in the world of advertising which was predominantly run by men.

On the other hand, when J.K. joined seven graduate trainee computer programmers at Esso Petroleum in 1967, five of them were women. However, that did not mean equality of pay, the two men receiving slightly higher salaries. When J.K. had started on her degree course in Philosophy at King's College, London, her parents must have wondered what sort of job that would lead to. They need not have worried.

Luckily, computer programmers were thin on the ground – no computer science or IT degrees in those days, otherwise I probably wouldn't have got the job (I had an aptitude test and interview). I remember drawing flowcharts with a plastic template, writing computer code on coding sheets with a pencil and sending them to the punch room where dozens of punch girls turned them into punched cards which came back in a box. (That cardpunch job does not exist any more.) We then took the box to the computer machine room which was full of tape drives, disk drives, and consoles – we weren't allowed in! Compiled the programme, did our test plans and created test data then put our programmes in for testing. Usually you got the results back the next day on that blue and white stripy concertina paper with sprocket holes down the side. These days, programmers type their code directly into their terminal and curse if it takes more than a minute to get their test results. We had IBM 360/50 and 360/65 mainframe computers. That meant 32k or 64k storage I think. (You probably have more than that on an I-phone these days.) Storage was precious – that is why dates were stored as yymmdd and not yyyymmdd thus creating the millennium bug scare. Nobody ever thought that COBOL programmes written in the 60s would still be running in 1999 – but they were! I was helping to maintain COBOL programmes as late as 2004.

That was the world of advanced technology into which another group of women were entering, those for whom the heading of life after school can be taken in its literal sense. These were the girls who at the opening of the decade were just beginning their secondary education, yet finished it either starting out on a career or getting married. It is surprising just how much of a life can be crammed into ten years when one is young. Yet these girls need to be considered as in many ways they represent much of what we think of as the Swinging Sixties. These are the girls who felt they had more freedom than their older sisters; who dared to rebel slightly against their parents' wishes – even if covertly; they were the ones who wholeheartedly embraced the music scene. Although they did not realise it at the time, they were the ones who would reap most of the benefit of being a teenager in the 1960s. H. grew up in Essex on the outskirts of London and in 1960 had just started an all-girls secondary modern school where she was introduced to the mysteries of algebra and geometry as well as having her love of history and English literature deepened. At thirteen she had to make the choice between taking the academic GCE course (which did not happen in all secondary moderns) or the commercial one, which included shorthand and typing. She ended up with CSE, RSA and Pitmans qualifications but before that, she was, in her own words, growing rapidly into a teenager.

I remember how the Mods and Rockers started. A lot of my friends at school had older sisters and they were becoming Mods. They were very smart – they all wore straight skirts with white T-shirts, on the back of which they put the initial of their first name in black. They also wore moccasin shoes and we younger one thought they were fantastic. For school we wore black lace ups. We nailed steel 'Blakeys' [small metal plates attached to the underside of shoes to correct wear in specific area] on the heels so when we walked our heels clicked. However, we were not allowed into the school assembly hall with these on, as they would have ruined the floor, so we had shoe inspection every morning. Make-up was not allowed either but we got round that. I remember mascara came in blocks that you spat on to achieve the Dusty Springfield look. My Dad hated it and kept saying 'get that muck off your face', but I still wore it. We all loved a lipstick from Max Factor called Pink Meringue, but it made you look like a corpse with black eyes and nearly white lips. We put eye shadow both on your lid and underneath your eyes. I could never do eyeliner, as I am left-handed and could not get a straight line, so I gave up. I later became a Mod, loving their fashion and music: The Beach Boys, the Rolling Stones, the Kinks, Dusty Springfield, the Four Seasons, Tamla Motown, Stevie Wonder ... and of course the Beatles – the Fab Four – everything was Fab in those days!

We shall hear more from H. later but reading her memories of her teens with its supervised youth clubs and Saturday night dances in the church hall where the girls got dressed up and brought along cakes and sandwiches to accompany the soft drinks in the interval, one wonders why the older generation was so concerned about this 'teenage revolution' which now seems so innocent. However, not everyone had such happy memories of her schooldays. F., too, attended a girls' Secondary Modern with a boys' school adjacent. There were strict rules regarding contact between the two, even to the extent of having different times for breaks and going home.

Secondary school was, I think, where I first became aware of the inequality for women in those days. We left at 15, the only examinations we took were RSA stage I and possibly Stage II in English and Arithmetic. The boys had the choice to stay on until 16 and take a range of GCE O Levels. There was very little choice for girls, although everyone could find work, as there were several large factories in the town. I decided to go to the Civic College and take a two–year secretarial course. I didn't really want to be a secretary but I didn't know what I did want to do! I enjoyed the college life even though I found typing and shorthand rather boring. But I was able to study on my own and gain O Level English Language and Literature. Again I found there were a lot of restrictions on those studying secretarial duties, for example we were expected to always wear skirts or dresses. This seemed unfair when observing the clothes worn by other students and I did lead a couple of rebellions about this matter!'

Although very aware of the inequalities of life for women at an early age, F. was at heart a very normal teenager of her time. Like most of them she listened in bed on Sunday nights to the Top Twenty on Radio Luxemburg. She would buy a record on a Saturday and play it continually until she bought the next one. F. recalled her Dansette record player on which it was possible to play either a stack of vinyl records one after the other, or by placing one record on the turntable and fixing the pick-up, it played that one over and over. Like other girls she went through phases from Cliff Richard until the Beatles came on the scene and eclipsed all the others. When they appeared live at her local Gaumont cinema she was there, screaming along with all the other girls. As an aside here, there is a lovely story of a family coming to London for the weekend. As a treat, father bought tickets for them to see a particular band they knew and liked. To their amazement, when a band they had not heard of, called the Beatles, appeared on stage, all the teenage girls sitting around them started screaming. The father stood up and asked them to all to be quiet, as he couldn't hear the music! The usually restrained F. started attending a youth club when she was fourteen, where there was dancing to records on most Saturday evenings but once a month they had a live band. Later she went to public dances, where occasionally there was trouble between rival Mods and Rockers, in which case she made sure she got away and went home. Incidentally, another contributor who happened to be spending the Easter weekend on the Essex coast maintains that the 'invasion' of the seaside town of Clacton by Mods and Rockers was greatly exaggerated by the Press. While youth clubs provided a valuable meeting place for those still at school, those who had ventured out to work and had some money to spend could meet up with friends in other places, preferably one with a juke box. For a description of what social life was like for those who lived outside London let us hear from J.M.

> Coffee bars were all the rage and Sudbury had three – the Zanzi Bar was great and a real meeting place. By day it was used by ladies out shopping, but from after school onward it was <u>the</u> place to meet. It had a jukebox and we would sit in there for hours, drinking hot blackcurrant and listening to Bob Dylan. At the weekend they would sometimes have a local live group playing in the Cellar – literally down a stepladder into a small cellar – a great atmosphere, but it would never be allowed now, as there was no escape route whatsoever. The other two coffee bars were The Bambi (meeting place for the Mods) and The Bongo (where the Rockers used to congregate). I was forbidden by my father ever to go into the Bongo, and much as I wanted to, I never did go in.

J.M.'s friend T. adds a few more details about these venues. 'The Bongo was where all the biker boys went, likewise the Bambi but the Zanzi Bar was run by Mrs Bird, whose husband the Revd. Brian Bird was a jazz fanatic.'

It became apparent from a number of recollections that quite often youth clubs were run by younger members of the clergy, among them the Revd David Sheppard, the former cricketer who later became Bishop of Liverpool. L. relates: 'On Thursday evening I used to go to a Youth Club called the 69 Club [at the Mayflower centre in Canning Town] run by David Sheppard. All the girls loved him, he was so very handsome and used to arrive on his motor bike in black leathers – very sexy.' The image of vicars riding motorcycles and running jazz evenings, possibly playing an instrument, epitomises the more relaxed attitudes of the younger clergy in the Sixties which realised that congregations were dwindling and it was important to engage with the young.

The term 'coffee bar' really came into being in the Sixties and in London and the bigger cities they were often purpose-built and equipped with bright Formica-topped tables and tubular chairs and Pyrex cups and saucers. In small provincial towns ordinary cafes and milk bars developed into coffee bars although as we see from the description of the Zanzi Bar they served several different types of clientele. They also served not only hot blackcurrant but hot lemon too. Both these were cheaper than coffee (which was of the instant variety) and a good alternative for those who did not drink coffee. Whatever they were drinking, the young people who congregated in them had come for, and found, companionship, conversation and music.

Chapter Two

Sex, Drugs and R ...

L egend would have it that sex was discovered in the 1960s! Quite how the world had managed to exist until that decade was never clearly explained. What really happened is that a series of events occurred that led to the subject being more publicly aired than it had been for the previous 150 years. The liberating moment for some came with an unusual lawsuit on the subject of censorship. Most people accepted that the morals of the country as a whole were guarded by careful screening of material which might have harmful effects on the general public. Every film shown in cinemas throughout the United Kingdom was preceded by a declaration that it had been passed by the British Board of Film Censors as being fit for public viewing. Theatrical performances and books were scrutinised in similar fashion to ensure that nothing outraged the sensibilities of audience or reader. But then it all changed.

Students and devotees of the books of Nottinghamshire's D. H. Lawrence had long been able to read the novel which, at a very basic level, reversed the usual romantic tale of girl from humble background who is courted by wealthy gentleman, by depicting a noble lady having an adulterous affair with a lowly worker on her husband's estate. Scandalous though that might be, to make matters worse, her betrayed husband had been crippled as a result of his active service in the First World War. The book was ahead of its time in openly examining the accepted rules of moral conduct of the day. However, the edition of *Lady Chatterley's Lover* that was on sale in British bookshops did not contain the full text as written by Lawrence and first published in 1928. That contained what were, for that time, explicit sex scenes and more importantly, used the crude, earthy language of the gamekeeper to describe the sex act. Illicit copies of the full text printed abroad had found their way into the country for years as had *The Life and Loves of Frank Harris, Fanny Hill* and others of that ilk. However, in August 1960 Penguin Books decided to bring a test case by printing a totally unexpurgated edition for sale in this country. The publishers were prosecuted under the 1959 Obscene Publications Act on the grounds that the book was liable to deprave or corrupt. The case was widely reported in the Press as a battle raged between those who seemed to belong to a fossilised generation, concerned with whether or not one would care for the book to be 'put into the hands of one's wife or servants' and the many eminent academics and writers who were called to testify to both the book's literary merit and the liberating effect it would have on literature in general. For the man in the street the case would have aroused little interest, but for the young and the curious, the salaciousness of the bits of the book that were read out in court made it something they longed to have – and if Penguin won their case, then the paperback edition would be available at a price they could afford.

The case, which ended in early November 1960, was a victory for Penguin. History was made that day and indeed many more did get to read the book, though it is doubtful if all the readers of *Lady Chatterley* went on to read Lawrence's other novels. It gained a reputation of being a 'naughty', 'dirty' or 'mucky' book, according to the strength of feeling of those who, without having read it, were firmly against it. Among those who did buy it, sadly, many found that it was only the sex scenes that really held their interest. Many of the copies confiscated for being read under the desk or inside another book jacket that found their way into the staff-rooms of secondary schools fell open at the much-thumbed pages containing the relevant scenes. It may well be an apocryphal story but for certain teenagers who were eager to read it but could not afford, or dared not buy their own copy, the problem was solved for them by the entrepreneurial young man in the Sixth Form who charged a sixpenny entry fee to his railway compartment and gave readings on the journey made to and from school. One contributor who was still at school at the time wrote: 'I always had my nose in a book. I can't actually remember what sort of thing I read. I can however, remember reading *Lady Chatterley's Lover* – only because of the court case, of course. It wasn't until years later that I re-read D. H. Lawrence properly.' Strangely the imposing edition of James Joyce's *Ulysses* had languished untouched on the shelves of a girls' school library for several years before a visiting young male scholar revealed the secrets of the thoughts of Molly Bloom. The book was promptly withdrawn before the girls could learn about Joyce's revolutionary use of the stream of consciousness.

In 1956, the American author Grace Metalious had produced a graphic bestselling novel about the inhabitants of Peyton Place. Made into a film the following year, this work was the forerunner of the serialisation which was shown in Britain on the new independent television channel, ABC, from 1964. *Peyton Place*'s dealing with explicit sexual themes shocked many viewers. That America should have contributed to the sexual revolution seems odd to those who are old enough to remember that in their films made in the 1940s, for example, one rarely saw a bedroom scene that featured a double bed occupied by two people; the exception being for the very old. Younger married couples were never shown in bed together; they always appeared to sleep in twin beds. For naïve adolescents – and a vast proportion of the population were still ill-informed with only the very basic knowledge of procreation – this must have caused even more confusion.

Sex education in most secondary schools was still a cause of embarrassment for both pupils and teachers. In the Fifties the subject was touched upon in the biology lesson that featured reproduction in rabbits. Perhaps the thought of the coupling of rabbits was intended to put young people off experimenting. In some secondary modern schools as well as lessons in cookery, needlework and laundry, girls were given lessons in child care but although a girl might be taught how to hold a plastic 'baby' to bath, feed or change its nappy, the vital information on the circumstances leading to finding herself having to do these things for real were never mentioned. Neither was any information given on the hormonal and emotional changes taking place in the bodies of both sexes. The expectation was that young people would remain innocent until marriage, so contraceptive measures were still not on open sale. Some schools did try to take a more realistic approach to dispensing information, usually by bringing in a medical expert to talk to certain age groups. This could work well. However, if the doctor were known to some of the pupils, this could cause embarrassment to the young people. In one girls' school, the girls aged thirteen and upward were encouraged to write down anonymously any questions they might have and place them in an envelope which hung on the notice board in their form room. The day before the doctor's talk, their form mistress discovered that the envelope was empty. Since she had a good rapport with her class she remarked that surely they had questions. Yes, they replied, they had, but they weren't sure how to put them into words. During the half-hour that followed, the young teacher (whose own knowledge of sex had been gained from literature and medical textbooks!) not only got the class clamouring to ask questions but she also did her best to answer them as frankly and as sensibly as she could. She was able, for example, to dismiss some of the old wives' tales they had already absorbed.

Following the *Lady Chatterley* case came a scandal which not only shocked the country, but also reinforced the belief of many that the upper classes were no better than they should be. The Press relished the now oft repeated story in television documentaries and in films, of wild parties in a famous country house, high-ranking members of the government, call girls and the shady dealings which involved both drugs and possible espionage. Reputations were ruined, careers shattered; and fifty years after the events, the names of Mandy Rice-Davies and Christine Keeler are still recalled.

So the sexual activities of others became a topic of conversation – and many ribald jokes. Then came another great scandal, that which again involved members of the upper class who were taken to court for homosexual practices. This was a subject which had probably not been discussed openly in this country since the time of Oscar Wilde. One might hear the names 'cissy', 'nancy boy' or even 'queer' applied, usually to someone who appeared effeminate but most young women had no idea of what homosexuality really meant. Indeed many girls found themselves with boyfriends who, they discovered in discussion with their friends, were very restrained in their advances towards them. Many thought this was merely a sign the young man had been brought up to respect women. When the couple married the girl, who had read books to prepare her for her honeymoon, was often very disappointed to discover that her new husband's response to her was rather muted. Many men, who tried to fight against their instinctive inclination, did indeed manage to father children and achieve a compatible relationship with their wives, but others were those, who, in middle age, took advantage of the change in the law to 'come out'.

The consequences for those young women whose first boyfriend was uncertain of his own sexuality could be disastrous. Brought up on a diet of romantic novels and films the fact that although he enjoyed her company, he made no attempt to do more than hold her hand and give her a peck on the cheek, led her to feelings of deep insecurity. What was wrong with her? Why didn't he fancy her? This often resulted in her being unable to have a normal relationship with any other man – until, that is, the knight in shining armour broke through her reserve and, in the words of a Barbara Cartland or Mills and Boon novel, 'awakened her very being'!

For the majority of young women in the first half of the 1960s however, they were well aware of normal sexual reactions to their boyfriends' advances, but they had been conditioned not to give in to them because 'nice girls didn't'. They had learned enough either from books or friends to know what could be the consequences and they did not want to run the risk of being that girl who suddenly disappeared from school or lecture room and became the subject of gossip. Somehow mothers instilled a fear into their daughters that such behaviour was not only wrong but if indulged in would not only ruin their own lives but would bring disgrace upon the whole family and might even lead to the girl being cast off and disowned by the family. Why risk that when you could bring 'your greatest gift' to a husband?

'As soon as I knew I was engaged and coming to the USA, all that "saving oneself" until marriage went out of the window'. So wrote B. who at nineteen arrived in a new country at the end of August 1963 already pregnant. Entirely unprepared for the life that was to follow, the reaction to her news was quite different to what it would have been in this country. 'We were married at the beginning of October. Couldn't do it sooner. We had to do the required "talk" with the minister and wait for licence and blood test results. This was Amish and Mennonite country. They had strict rules. But nobody judged me for being pregnant. Seems it was quite common!' In an earlier account B who had left school at fifteen, had described her social life: 'My friends and I went to all the coffee bars, and at seventeen I was going in pubs. Nobody checked my age – I was out every night. On Sundays we went up to London and to the seaside in the summer. We had dates, but never sex.'

It is interesting that B. believed that once she had an engagement ring this was a guarantee of marriage and therefore it was quite in order to begin marital relations. In a way, she was following the age-old custom of betrothal; and in her native Suffolk, there was a time when a child on the way before the actual marriage service was taken as a good sign, proving that the woman was fertile. It is however doubtful that in 1960s Suffolk her parents would have taken the same view. There were, however, others who followed the same thinking, among them L.A. describing her life in the early 1960s.

> I used to go to Stratford Town hall dances on a Saturday night with a friend. We had a great time meeting boys, but things were quite innocent then, not like today when all they seem to think about is jumping into bed with any Tom, Dick or Harry. There were a few girls who put themselves about a bit, had sex and boasted about it but they were just known as sluts and you steered clear of them because you really didn't want to be tarred with the same brush. I can remember going out with a boy who wanted me to have sex with him but if you were a decent girl you just didn't. My first time I had sex I was 17 and engaged to be married.

Not all the contributors gave a specific answer to the question about their sexual activity during the 1960s but one might be forgiven for thinking that as the so-called Swinging Sixties progressed towards the end of the decade that there would have been a more relaxed attitude to pre-marital sex. Yet the following do not support that view.

> It was unthinkable to live with a man unless you were married to him so we married in 1966. J.K.
>
> Sex? Yes, there was plenty of opportunity but I think I must have been a bit of a goody-two-shoes (or possibly just scared of getting pregnant) because the only chap I slept with was the one I eventually married. Lots of my friends claimed to be having sex, whether they were or not, I don't know. (Apart from the one or two that got pregnant – it's fair to say they weren't making it up.) T., 1968.
>
> In 1968 I was working in London, sharing a flat with a friend from home. We went to parties ... I did not do the sex thing – still the prim and proper public school girl who wanted to wait for true love.

J.B. then added, 'I did not get married until 1992 – when I was forty-three years old – a very late starter who wanted to get it right!' 'We went out together for three years and were married in 1970. We would never have lived together before we were married – it just was not done'.

So what about those who 'did' and got caught out, as J. did in 1967? She wrote quite honestly; 'We did experiment with sex as I'm sure most teenagers have done over the years. We also smoked and drank alcohol before we were eighteen. I got married at eighteen in the Registry office as I was expecting my son. My wedding dress cost £5 and our reception was in my parents' front room; we had the Sunday in Yarmouth, then back to work on the Monday.' She was one of the lucky ones in so far as she had the support of her parents, not just through the pregnancy but she and her new husband lived with them until the baby was eight months old and they were able to rent a place on their own.

It was a very different story for High School girl H.P. She had taken her GCE exams and was to enter the Sixth Form after the summer holidays which she spent working in the kitchen of a seaside hotel. It was not long before she found herself attracted to the nineteen-year-old French waiter. H.P., like many of the girls at the time who had been educated in girls' schools, was naïve; she says now that she does not remember ever having talks about sex either at home or at school. As far as she was concerned the whole thing was mysterious and embarrassing. But telling the young man that she was not a virgin and that she could not get pregnant, they spent the summer having sex; the act itself she didn't find exciting but she enjoyed the intimacy involved. Reading her account one forms the impression that tenderness was lacking in her family. This was borne out when the inevitable happened and on a fateful day in September the young man went with her to tell her parents. Her mother received the news very badly and promptly rang her father who came home and in true melodramatic form threw the boy out of the house before sending H.P. to the chemist to get something to calm her mother who, presumably, was having hysterics! All contact with the boy was forbidden. Meantime H.P. went miserably to school each day, started her A level course knowing she would not continue with it and indeed she left at the end of that term, just seventeen. The reaction of H.P.'s mother was perhaps typical of many middle-class women with the desire to keep the whole thing a secret especially as her elder daughter was due to get married and such a scandal could not be allowed to spoil the bride's big day. So that wedding was brought forward so that H.P. could be a bridesmaid, for her not to have been her sister's attendant would have been remarked upon by friends and family, not to mention the neighbours. Once Christmas was over – and one can imagine it was a pretty cheerless one – H.P. was sent to stay with her brother who was living in the army base at Catterick with his young wife. They were kind to her but very much wrapped up in each other. She went with them when they were posted to Wales where her baby was born. She concluded her story: 'I don't know what excuses my parents made to their families but nothing was ever said and my baby boy was adopted. I did not feel I had any say in the matter. I felt nothing for a very long time.'

Similar stories occurred all over the country and to girls from different walks of life. An early termination had never been an option since medical abortion was only legalised in 1969 and then only when certain requirements, such as the threat to mental or physical health of the mother, were met. For those who had the money to pay for it there were discreet but illegal, medically supervised clinics in London and possibly in other large cities. There were also what were known as back-street abortionists who ran the risk of legal proceedings if they were caught. Horrendous stories circulated about the results of botched terminations, which resulted in permanent damage to the woman or even death. Unsupervised attempts to bring about a miscarriage by sitting in a very hot bath and drinking gin were so graphically described in novels and films of the period, such as *Saturday Night and Sunday Morning*, they were enough to frighten most girls who found themselves pregnant. If the young man responsible had disappeared from the scene or if both parties were under the legal age to marry and one or other set of parents objected to a marriage, then that left only two ways to deal with the situation. They could allow the girl to keep the baby and absorb it into the family, thus creating the situation where a child grew up believing his grandmother was his mother, when in fact his elder sister was his real mother. Alternatively, and at that time the more usual answer, was to have the baby adopted. There has been sufficient publicity and television programmes highlighting the sometimes harsh treatment that existed in Mother and Baby Homes to make it unnecessary to go into detail here. Fortunately, some of those like H.P. were reunited many years later with their child, while those who were not should gain some comfort in knowing that in most cases, their child was given a loving home by a couple who were unable to have children.

Reading or listening to material about the 1960s one could easily gain the impression that until the newly-developed contraceptive pill was available women had to rely totally on their partner to use a condom. These had been on sale for a number of years but not, it has to be said, on open sale even in the chemist's shop. Manufactured and discreetly packaged mainly by the firm trading as Durex, one of the biggest dispensers was the old-fashioned barber shop where, after having his hair cut, the client might be asked if 'he required anything for the weekend'. But condoms were not always reliable and often men either did not bother to use them or could not afford to buy them. By the 1920s the rising birth rate amongst the poorer members of society was giving great concern, bringing as it did problems of severe overcrowding, poor nutrition and infantile diseases, early child deaths and worse, the high maternal mortality of women who died in giving birth to yet another child, leaving perhaps as many as ten others who almost inevitably would end up in a children's home. The campaigner Marie Stopes decided the time had come to do something about it and in 1921 she set up her first clinic, in London, to give advice to married woman on what they could do to regulate their pregnancies. By 1930 the Ministry of Health had recognised the problem by giving power to Local Authorities to provide birth control advice to married women for whom a further pregnancy would prove detrimental. However, even when the National Health Service was introduced in 1946, it did not include the provision of free Family Planning advice. That came later. But for the time being it was possible for married woman to be fitted with one of several internal contraceptive devices. Where did that leave the woman who was about to start married life but for various reasons did not wish to become pregnant straight away? The answer nowadays would be to take the Pill if she was not already doing so but alas, the much vaunted Pill was not available to every woman. Trials had begun in 1961 but as we have seen with other innovations, they did not happen overnight or all over the country. Many general practitioners were not only reluctant to prescribe it when it did become more widely available but actually refused to do so. The Roman Catholic Church forbade any type of contraception except for what was known as 'the safe period' in a woman's menstrual cycle – a practice which was as unreliable as the regularity of some women's cycle. But it was not just RC doctors who had to follow the teachings of the Church: others opposed the idea on moral and ethical grounds, while others who were set in their ways just did not agree with interfering with nature.

It is interesting to learn the different attitudes and experiences women of the 1960s had to family planning. When she married in 1965 one was determined that married life would not interfere with her quest to complete her education and secure a good job. She also believed that she had to make up for all the opportunities she had missed as a teenager to enjoy a cultural life and to travel, so she went on the pill until such time as she and her husband felt ready to start a family, their first child arriving some six years later. How different for the woman who was twenty-six when she had her first child in 1957, the second two years later and then, having got them off to school and thinking of returning to work, after a gap of five years a third arrived in 1964 followed by number four under two years later. She was sterilised after that. That may seem a drastic form of birth control but the procedure was usually performed only for medical reasons and then it had to be with the husband's consent.

Contraception was not straightforward. Before I left London [to live in Wales], I had been told by a friend that she had had a Dutch cap fitted. Although her wedding was booked and imminent, the doctor peppered the cap with holes to prevent it being used prematurely. I imagined the 'pill', which was well established by 1969, to be the answer. The health implications were being debated but I decided to go ahead. The nurse who examined me was rude and the doctor's finger nails so grimy that I supposed she had spent the day in the garden. She prescribed the pill but within days I had become so breathless I could not get up the hill to our house.

Although possibly hailed by some as the answer to the prayers of every woman of childbearing age, the use of the pill was indeed controversial. It was the subject of debate not only amongst medical and religious groups, it was a topic that was discussed and agonised over, by the mothers of women about to be married who were particularly concerned that it had not been in use long enough to discover what its long-term side effects might be. There was talk of it being likely to induce thrombosis, so anyone who had a family history of that was warned to be careful. Then it was supposed to encourage weight gain or induce mood swings. Those women who suffered any unusual reaction, as in the case quoted above, were likely to pass the information on to others. This wariness of taking a comparatively new drug, which was in any way connected to changing the pattern of women's reproductive system, was to some extent explained by what had happened with the drug thalidomide, which in the 1950s was heralded as the panacea for severe morning sickness in early pregnancy. The worst of all possible long-term side effects emerged when the first of the severely-disabled babies appeared, born to mothers who had taken the drug.

As a young nurse I married in 1964. I must admit I was as green as grass about family planning. There was no way I would have asked my mother or sister for advice. But some of the older nurses were more ready to give advice (not always helpful). It was never discussed openly but more likely to be in small groups hidden away in the sluice, talking quietly. The general opinion was that the 'pill' was a bit dangerous; maybe causing blood clots or strokes (highly unlikely), but the Press had had a field day with their scare stories. I was to learn that one of the hospital doctors held a private clinic, fitting Dutch caps. It cost about £2.0.0 for a visit which was arranged for a few days before the wedding. This clinic was held in a private house in the town. Quite a full examination took place with lots of questions being asked about family history etc. It was not an easy visit. But this was a successful method which allowed us to plan our families. Some of my nursing friends did choose to take the 'pill', which later became the method of choice alongside the coil.

I feel that women very quickly became aware of what was available, and clinics were held in the GP's surgery. The advice I would give to anyone who asked me for family planning was to contact the surgery. [Following her marriage S.T. became a district nurse.] This being a rural area I do not remember there being a separate clinic in the 1960s. A patient would have to travel to Barrow in Furness some twenty miles away to visit a Family Planning Clinic, where they felt that no one would know their business. Advice was also given at the postnatal clinic and before discharge from the maternity wards.

Yes, I used the pill. It made a fantastic difference. [Like many teenagers in the latter half of the 1960s who were in a steady relationship this girl and her boyfriend enjoyed 'making love', though she admitted that her worst nightmare was becoming pregnant and having to give up her career.] I was too shy to go to my own doctor so just before the wedding, I went to my future husband's doctor and he said it was a jolly good idea. I took it for a year, but was repeatedly ill, so the specialist I saw said I should not take it any longer. I believe that the early contraceptive pills had a vast quantity of oestrogen in them compared to those today. But for me, using the pill was fun while it lasted!

That woman was lucky in finding an understanding doctor. J.T. had a more trying experience when using a Family Planning Clinic before her wedding in 1966.

The pill had just come out and I will never forget the indignity of having to queue up in the street in Harlow outside the clinic to get to be seen by the Family Planning people. Every man that drove past blew his car horn and yelled out. Queue baiting seemed to be a popular sport for the local male populace! Even then, I was so naïve that I burst into tears when they said that they had to examine me before they would dish out the pills. I was a virgin as I had paid heed to all the dire warnings about 'not getting into trouble'. Nobody used the word sex in those days and it was considered to be the ultimate sin to get pregnant out of wedlock. Not a very good start to married life.

Dr A. throws some light on the subject from the perspective of a young female doctor who entered a northern general practice in 1957.

Ideas were quite different then and such things were not generally discussed. I did discuss contraception at my post-natal visits. One of my female colleagues fitted diaphragms – Dutch Caps. Most advice was about condoms, coils, 'safe periods' and the new oral contraceptives becoming known as the 'pills'. Many of us [in the medical profession] were concerned about thrombosis and side effects over a long period of time. It was quite a new idea to discuss family planning. One of my male colleagues had a Roman Catholic female partner who was quite offended when he asked her if she wanted advice.

Dr A. went on to say that she did not do her family planning training which involved prescribing the pill and fitting coils and so on until the 1970s, so what follows while not the 1960s, does show very neatly why better forms of contraception were needed. 'One of my patients, a mother of ten, brought two of her daughters aged sixteen and seventeen and said, "Doc – put them on the pill and give them a choice – I never had one!"'

Had the pill been readily available to all who requested it, would the 1960s women have taken advantage of it to have premarital sex not just with their future partner but also with any man who asked? An earlier contributor called herself naïve (as indeed were many of the other women) and one might be forgiven for thinking that perhaps she had led a very sheltered life, yet this was not the case. She and her school friends had met up with boys after school and at the weekends and in the summer of 1962, she even went on holiday with her boyfriend. 'We went for a week's youth hostelling on Dartmoor. Youth Hostelling was considered a respectable activity as the boys and girls had separate dorms and there could be no fraternisation! It rained all the time and I nearly died of exhaustion and hypothermia so I did not repeat the experience.' This girl spent her further education years surrounded by males with whom she felt on equal terms and she also had a steady boyfriend. Yet throughout all that time she was able to maintain her virginity.

Nor was she alone in this. Another fifteen-year-old who belonged to a youth club which allowed her to mix with a variety of boys, some of whom had what she called 'zany' friends, recalled that she was taken for a ride on the back of a motorbike, minus a helmet, of course, by a young man anxious to share with her the thrill of 'doing a ton' along the local by-pass. Young as she was she recognised the danger she could be in, if she continued their acquaintance: 'His strong sex drive, fast friends and a habit of being imaginative with the truth was too much and we drifted apart.' Which raises the question of why was it that some girls did and others did not? In 1963 when this girl was sixteen and 'going steady' with another boy, she and a girlfriend were invited by her boyfriend's mother to spend a holiday on the south coast in her caravan. She discovered there were lots of other young people on the site and, in her words, 'regular orgies took place in some caravans. I could not stomach the sight of so many bodies crammed together, all having sex at once, so I left without becoming involved. I seem to remember that we preferred doing the twist in the ballroom.'

There is some evidence to suggest that attitudes towards premarital sex had changed during the latter part of the decade though this was not due to the use of the Pill; in fact most unmarried couples relied entirely upon condoms, (as did a large proportion of married couples.) This is not the place for digging deeply into what caused the upsurge in sexual activity; in part it may be due to the fact that sex was discussed more openly or that after years of being told it was wrong to yield one's virginity before marriage, many women began to question why they should hang on to it, especially if they really loved someone. R.A. was in her early twenties and working in a London bank where she met a customer, a young African studying Law on a scholarship from Rhodesia (as it was then). They were attracted to each other and started going out. Because he was so far from home she invited him to spend Christmas at the home she shared with her father and brother. (Her mother had died the year before.) R.A. did not make this clear but it is likely that it was at this time she became pregnant. When she told her father, he was 'reasonably OK about it. I think he was worried about our future and how the outside world would view us. He had a talk with my boyfriend about his intentions. I think his parents were shocked when he told them and I remember them being a bit cross that they thought he'd abused our hospitality. We got married in March 1969. I was twenty-three and he was twenty-five. We lived in a flat for six months but moved back to the family home before our son was born in September.' R.A.'s father's reaction to her condition was quite liberal for the time. He did not immediately throw her out as some might have done but he was very concerned at the prospect of his daughter being in a mixed-race marriage, expressed in those words 'how the outside world would view us'. However, R.A. also reveals the reaction of the young man's parents – they were shocked and they were cross. It was revealed that both his parents were highly educated, with his father playing an important role in the political life of his country. No doubt the situation presented to them was not the future they had foreseen for their son. R.A. reported that while her friends were very supportive, she did not think her new husband's friends approved of the marriage. The pressures were such that the marriage did not last long.

One of the hackneyed tags applied as a subtitle for the 1960s is 'Sex, Drugs and Rock'n'Roll'. Having discovered that sex was not quite as rampant as we have been led to believe, it is time to discover what impact the drugs scene had on those whose lives we have been studying. Again, if you believe the myths, drug use, like sex, began in the Sixties. One only has to look back to nineteenth-century literature to realise that this was not so. There was a time when every school pupil knew the story of how the poet Coleridge was writing his poem *Kubla Khan* under the influence of opiates when he was interrupted by a visitor, the man from Porlock, and afterwards was unable to recapture the dream induced vision. Later, the novels of Dickens and others provided vivid descriptions of men driven to visit opium dens, while Conan Doyle hints that the drug heightened Sherlock Holmes' powers of deduction. Laudanum in tincture form was widely used as a painkiller amongst the upper classes, particularly women, and nursemaids were known to put a drop or two into a teething baby's feed, sometimes with fatal results.

Drug use continued into the twentieth century but the so-called explosion in the 1960s was noticeable because it was no longer the preserve of the moneyed class. Increasing prosperity, as we have already seen, meant that the 'Them' and 'Us' divide was becoming blurred and those who previously had no contact with drugs were being offered the chance to experiment and live 'like They do', even if it was only for a while. But just as the contraceptive pill was not immediately accessible to all, so it took time for drug taking to become widespread amongst the young.

At the beginning of the decade, Dr A. noted: 'Alcohol was a bigger problem than drugs in our area in 1960 but young people did refuse cigarettes from strangers at dances in case they had drugs in them.'

I can honestly say I never came into contact with drugs ... I was forbidden by my father ever to go into the Rockers Coffee bar and much as I wanted to, I never did. At the weekends there were often house-parties and we would go as a group, taking some drink with us and just arrive, often uninvited, but that seemed to be acceptable at the time. I was never a great drinker, which was just as well, as I was usually driving a car full of friends – of course there were no drink driving laws back then.

Alcohol was a feature at parties though we had no money so only got some if someone else was paying.

Every Saturday there would be at least one party to go to. Rooms would be always very smoky [from cigarettes] so Sundays were spent with very sore eyes. Drink was taken, but not to excess. I remember the party when everyone brought a bottle of Emva Cream sherry as it was on special offer at the local off-licence.

We didn't drink or take drugs and to be honest never really came across that.

We usually had wine and whisky and sherry at home at Christmas. My first real alcoholic drink was a sip of gin and orange [This would have been orange squash.]

I never came across drugs at all. We had no Arts faculty – maybe engineering types were not of the romantic, spiritual persuasion. I don't know. However, I went to lots of parties held by students from the Music College and they were also completely drug free. We didn't drink a lot. We could only afford one lager to last all evening or the occasional rum and coke.

Went to various parties – can't say I noticed much of drugs scene – it was there, but hardly wild! Plenty of alcohol though.

'No sign of drugs'. All the above statements refer to the years between 1960 and 1965 when it would appear that drink was most likely to provide any stimulation a party needed – and that was in much smaller quantities than are consumed nowadays. Most young people did not have the money to buy bottles of alcohol which, in any case, were only available on sale in off-licenses during licensing hours which again, were much more restricted than those of the twenty-first century. However, things changed slightly during the second half of the decade. Drug-taking was talked about amongst young people who grasped the significance of the clues given in the songs of the time. It came as a shock to many mothers who had happily sung *Puff, the Magic Dragon* along with their small children to be told that it might have referred to smoking marijuana or that the Beatles' *Lucy in the Sky with Diamonds* was a reference to LSD.

There certainly were drugs about, at parties etc. although no one ever directly offered me any. A friend remarked to me that I shouldn't bother to try pot because there was nothing to it and therefore no reason to take more. Wise words. Another friend thought he could fly from an upstairs landing at a party – he 'd probably been taking LSD – but I was so shocked and upset at seeing him like that that it was a great incentive never to touch drugs at all. So I didn't.

Drugs passed me by as did smoking.

We went to parties and occasionally I was aware that we were offered cannabis, but I did not partake. Nor did I do the sex thing – still the prim and proper public school girl who wanted to wait for true love.

Alcohol wasn't a very important part of our lives. Neither were drugs. I guess there were drugs around, but certainly between leaving school in 1963 and getting married in 1969 they were not as widely available as they were in the 70s.

Sex and drugs were not much in evidence [in 1968]. There were rumours of 'funny cigarettes' and one of our year may have smoked one. The pub was one of our social outings. A favourite was The Ship, its claim to fame was that it was said to have been Sir Francis Drake's favourite too. It had an open fire so was warm and we worked out it was cheaper to buy half a pint of shandy and make it last all evening than feed the gas meter in the digs.

In our second year (1969) of nursing training we were allowed to move out of the Nurses home and I shared a house with five other nurses. One of them used to take uppers and downers but I wasn't interested. I knew LSD was around but with my deep and ever present sadness I felt I could not chance it in case it sent me mad.

I didn't come into contact with any kind of drugs until 1970 when I had a boyfriend who smoked cannabis, so I did too.

Although the above contributor confessed to smoking cannabis, one suspects it was rather a case of bravado than anything else. However, there is no doubt that many women would be horrified to know that they could be classified as 'drug users' or even worse, addicts, in the 1960s. Yet such is the case, as the words of another song of the period has it, they were those who used 'mother's little helpers' to get them through the day. Here is not the place to examine why so many women felt depressed – or stressed – at the time or why doctors were so quick to prescribe Valium to help them by day or Librium to calm their nerves and help them sleep. They also readily prescribed amphetamines, the so-called 'pep pills', both as a slimming aid as well as a pick-me-up for those who felt the need of such. One contributor, a teacher in a tough school in one of the ports told of how, having put on weight after her marriage, she had asked her doctor if he could prescribe an appetite suppressant. One day in class her handbag fell to the floor, opened and some of the contents, including her bottle of tablets fell out. The helpful boy who rescued the items looked carefully at the bottle before handing it back, then much to her horror offered her sixpence for each of the tablets. She then abandoned her prepared lesson while she allowed the class to educate her on drugs, their use, their sale value and much more. She maintains that she learnt more about real life among teenagers at that school than she ever taught them! Slowly the habit and the drugs were making inroads into everyday life as the Sixties drew to a close and we drifted toward the Seventies in a smoke-filled haze to begin its own myths as 'the Hippy Era'.

So what about that third subject, the R … in the title? Some will assume that this should be for 'Rock'n'Roll' but that has been dealt with elsewhere. The R … here follows on from drugs, looking at what Karl Marx described as 'the opium of the people', that is, religion. From the evidence offered, it would be safe to assume that at the beginning of the Sixties most of the women questioned had been brought up at least as nominal Christians. Some belonged to families who had a strong allegiance to one or other branch of the Church. The girls from these families regularly attended services on Sundays, perhaps becoming part of the choir or a Sunday School teacher as well as taking part in the church's weekday activities. Their friends tended to come from the church congregation and it was likely they would marry someone who practised the same beliefs, as was the case for S.T., D. and M. For each of these women their faith has remained an integral part of their lives. Other families were more lax; they may have sent their children to the local Sunday School but for the most part the Church was there mainly for weddings, christenings and funerals – and even that was changing as more people were opting for cremation.

Change had also come to schools. Under the terms of the 1944 Education Act every state school had to have a daily act of nondenominational religious worship. This was a formal occasion which featured a hymn, a Bible reading and prayers. The solemnity might then be broken as the head teacher addressed the school about some infringement of rules or important announcement but it did mean that every schoolchild absorbed, almost by osmosis, a knowledge of a range of hymns as well as a chance to hear readings from, at that time, the King James Bible. Parents had a right to withdraw their child from Assembly on religious grounds, so Roman Catholics, Jews and some other strict religious sects did not attend the religious part of daily assembly. As the large comprehensives came into being, so it was unlikely that there was room in the assembly hall, which often doubled as the gymnasium, to accommodate all the pupils. So smaller assemblies were held, sometimes at different times of the day and with increasing diversity within the population, the whole character of the assembly changed too.

While many of the parents of our 1960s women may have given up on church-going it is interesting to note that most of their daughters, who had themselves rarely gone to church while they were living away from home, returned home for a church wedding. More surprising perhaps is the reaction of M.H.'s parents when in 1966 at the age of sixteen she announced she had become a committed Christian, which was probably influenced by the London Crusade by the American evangelist Billy Graham in that year.

And thereafter my social life mainly revolved around Church youth clubs and my Sunday Girl Crusaders class; activities that were grudgingly tolerated by my parents – they were afraid I might become 'too religious'. Once at University I had a boyfriend whom I met through the Christian Union, this relationship was severely frowned on by my parents as I was supposed to be at University to work, not getting involved with boys. By the end of 1969 I met another Christian Union member through a mutual friend and we married in 1975, again with much opposition from my parents in the early days.

The 1960s was definitely a defining decade for established religion; the Roman Catholic Church's Second Vatican Council (1962–5) was an attempt to modernise some teachings in order to stem the decline in congregation numbers as well as a shortage of candidates for the priesthood. The Anglican Church, too, tried to overcome dwindling congregations by making services more relevant to modern life. While the established church suffered, there was a rise in membership among the free churches and in particular of certain sects. At a time when the country generally was becoming more liberal in its outlook perhaps it was a natural reaction that those who did not like what they saw should turn to churches, which shunned the 'evils' of modern life. The Church of the Latter Day Saints or Mormons which had had a small base in the United Kingdom since late Victorian times, suddenly flourished in the Sixties as converts accepted the rigours of foregoing all stimulants, cigarettes and accepted chastity before marriage. The Jehovah's Witnesses, Plymouth Brethren and Seventh Adventists also found many new followers. Most non-churchgoers happily went on as they always had done, but for others, particularly the young there were other options to explore. The Beatles influenced many to explore mysticism through the practice of Zen Buddhism, Yoga, Sufism and Transcendental Meditation, all of which were paving the way to the idea of Peace and Love in the Seventies.

Chapter Three

Marriage – the Hidden Agenda

While reading through the accounts of girls who had chosen to go to university, which presupposed that they were intending to follow a career, R.'s sentence, 'Along with most of my friends, "the hidden agenda" then was finding partners and settling down', came as a surprise. The contributor continued: 'Despite being able to live independently – I shared flats with various friends and we went to and gave many parties – marriage and a family (early) was the ultimate ideal I think, with many friends subsequently resuming good careers after spending time at home.'

A pattern had been emerging that the girls who left school at fifteen or sixteen often married before they were twenty and started a family straight away. It also appeared that some of these early marriages were an attempt to escape from parental control and gain freedom. For some it worked, but many found that life as a married woman was even more restrictive. A question that is difficult to answer is why did so many girls of that era feel so out of touch with their parents? Time and again, contributors referred to their parents, mothers especially, as being very strict with them. We all know that the young go through a stage of rejecting everything their parents stand for but many of the Sixties girls did not dare let their rebellious feelings show and so appeared malleable to maternal manipulation. Was it that these mothers, who were so strict, were those who had been young in the 1940s and, remembering how they had behaved, wished to prevent their daughters making mistakes? Possibly. Or was it that these women, who had shouldered all the responsibility of the family while their husbands had been away throughout the war, found it difficult to settle down again to having a man controlling their lives, so unwittingly tried to control their children? A good example of the controlling mother was M.O.'s. Having dictated what courses she should take at school, she also interfered in M.O.'s relationships with boys, finding fault with any that showed interest in her daughter. That is until she 'semi-approved of P.'. He was older than M.O. but as he was the younger brother of her mother's friend, he was encouraged. M.O., seeing marriage as her chance to escape from home, accepted his proposal. However, unbeknown to her, the fiancé asked his prospective father-in-law if the newly-weds could rent the flat over the family's shop. M.O. was furious when she heard this. It was the last thing she wanted: 'More than anything I wanted to get away from home, away from my very strict mother.' The couple had a row and the engagement was broken off. Her mother greeted the news with horror; the honeymoon had been booked, all the preparations for the wedding made and presents had started arriving. Two weeks passed and the erstwhile fiancé turned up with a new plan for their future housing and M.O. was persuaded to go along with that – and the wedding. Greatly to her mother's relief, they would not have to return all the presents! And, one suspects, neither would she have to bear the indignity of explaining a cancelled wedding to friends and neighbours.

It is ironic that in recent years when marriage became unfashionable and couples have not only lived together but produced a family, that weddings have now become very elaborate and costly events. Convention was such that 1960s woman would not have considered living with her boyfriend; in fact she would found it well-nigh impossible to do so. Quite apart from momentous parental disapproval, it would have been difficult to find accommodation that would have accepted them without their having to lie and build a fictitious background for themselves. It was a brave – or brazen – couple, who attempted even a weekend away together; the 'soi disant, Mr and Mrs Smith' had to weather suspicious glances from the hotel clerk and remember to answer to that name, while the young woman had to make sure she was wearing the wedding ring hastily bought from Woolworths. Feelings of guilt spoilt much of the pleasure, so it was better to wait and get married.

Convention may have precipitated some marriages, but the 1960s brides did not necessarily follow it where wedding dresses were concerned. In the Fifties one could more or less guess exactly what the bridal dress would look like, what sort of bouquet would be carried and what form the 'going-away outfit' would take. But the Sixties changed that and it became the era of rising and falling hemlines. In 1960 M.O. wore a calf-length ballerina dress that she made herself. 'The dress was made of scalloped white lace and brocade with a full skirt over a stiff petticoat. The lace was quite expensive to buy but I made it for about a quarter of the cost to buy a readymade. I wore white leather shoes with pointy toes and carried a white prayer book and a red rose.'

M.O. also made the bridesmaids' dresses. A year later G. had what she describes as a very economical wedding with only twenty-nine guests. Her stepmother made her dress from material that cost £3.0.0. At the time the average price for a wedding dress was £20.0.0. S.M.'s wedding in 1965 was also done on a shoestring. She too, made her own dress; being just over thirty she opted for a traditional style with a small train and long sleeves that came to a point over her hands. The cream brocade cost £5.0.0; the material for short cream veil cost just over one pound and on the day it was held in place by a one and sixpenny (1/6d) plastic Alice band from Woolworths covered with a scrap of the dress material and studded with small pearls from a broken necklace. She also made trousers and waistcoats in dark brown corduroy for her two small pages, both of whom were most upset when, their father having told them they would be carrying a train, they discovered they had been seriously misled.

One of the most expensive items for S.M.'s dress was the long back zip. Zips were notoriously difficult to put in so when S.T.'s sister made her dress from white flock satin that cost 2/6d per yard, she opted to use the newly-available Velcro instead of a zip to fasten the back of the dress. 'This proved to be the wrong thing to do, as during the reception one of my little nieces stood on the train of my dress. The Velcro gave way, my dress opened right down the back leaving one bride half naked in front of the amused guests.' If that wasn't embarrassment enough, while on their honeymoon in the Lake District (actually not far from home for them) the young couple attended Sunday service at the local Baptist church. 'During the very long and boring sermon I must have dropped off to sleep, as my new bright yellow pillbox hat [came off] and rolled all the way down the aisle – with my new husband rushing to retrieve it!'

Some contributors mentioned their mothers making their dresses and those of the bridesmaids too. Only one of these women was trained and had during the 1930s worked as a couturier dressmaker. She had retained her love of fine clothes, choosing the best of materials she could afford and her daughter had benefited from her mother's taste and skill. Having made wedding dresses for various members of her family and friends, she was to take great pleasure in making her only daughter's wedding dress about which W. had very strong ideas of what she wanted. It was to be a February wedding so she chose 'a straight dress and coat in oyster coloured wild silk. The coat had a stand up collar and a high waist, fastened at the front with covered buttons. The coat opening fell away in a curve to a small train. The dress was simple with no details. A headband of orange blossom held a full-length veil in place. The two bridesmaids wore coat dresses in a similar style in magenta dupion.' W.'s comment on the dress beneath the coat being plain 'so I was able to hide a vest underneath' shows an eminently practical streak, though it is not clear if it was hers or her mother's!

Other mothers simply used skills they had learned through practice, and often, necessity. There was a time when most households possessed a sewing machine and when ready-made items were reasonably expensive, it was much cheaper to buy material and a pattern and make your own whether it be a dress, a coat, a pair of curtains or turning sheets sides to middle, the latter custom dying out with the introduction of nylon sheets. Our 1960s girls may have had some instruction in needlework at school, but most of them felt confident enough to run up a dress for themselves, even if not all of them were prepared to take on the wedding dress. There were, however, other options available for those who did not have access to a skilled needlewoman; R., who was working in London, hired her dress, a long Empire line coat style of lace over taffeta with a long veil, as did L.A., also a Londoner, described her dress as being 'of an "A" line style under the bust, lacy with three quarter sleeves with pearl drops on the bodice and the two bridesmaids, who were a school friend and a work friend, wore turquoise three quarter sleeved "A" line dresses which were also hired'.

Unfortunately, there is no record of hire costs but they cannot have been too expensive. L. bought her dress from John Lewis in Oxford Street for 22 guineas (£23.2s.0d). Strangely L. does not describe her dress but she did remember that her going-away outfit 'was a smart costume with a flowery yellow hat and matching accessories'. Yellow was obviously the fashionable colour for hats, probably not worn again except for visits to church but the smart suit would certainly be taken into service for work in the same way as a new winter coat worn to go on honeymoon would probably replace the bride's best coat, allowing the existing one to become everyday wear.

Then there were those women who chose to be different. D., who returned to be married in the Methodist church in her hometown, wore a white silk kaftan with a short veil. This was 1968 and the emerging influence of the Hippy movement. D.'s comment on her dress was 'my mother was not impressed'. J.K., on the other hand, turned her back on any of the frills associated with weddings, unlike the rest of the girls in her year who had gone to university in London and returned home for a traditional-style ceremony. Her account stands out because it was not only so very different but shows the independent spirit that was growing within 1960s women.

> Got married July 1965 [that was the end of her first year at University] at St Pancras Town Hall – I think I walked there – in a blue suit. Can't remember what the licence cost. Mum had sent £5.0.0. towards an outfit which I spent on tickets for the Kirov Ballet at the Festival Hall. Both sets of parents came to the wedding – Dad took a photo or two afterwards – it was raining. Had lunch afterwards at the Imperial Hotel, Russell Square – my Dad paid. In the evening went – without parents – to Hammersmith Odeon to see *The Knack* (Rita Tushingham). After working through the summer at London University checking A Level results – clerical job no brain power required but £9.0.0 a week – we flew to Oslo, Norway booked through NUS [National Union of Students] for two weeks coming back by boat from Bergen to Newcastle.

What a contrast the lunch for six at a London hotel was to most wedding receptions. Between fifty to sixty guests assembled at the Grand Hotel in Weymouth for L.'s reception, which she said 'was quite fun'. She does not give details but we assume that it was a luncheon and that her father paid for the affair.

> We all went back to my parent's house afterwards for me to change – and then one of Alec's college friends drove us down to the railway station to get the train to London. I remember my friends scattering confetti all over us and writing 'Just Married' in lipstick on the train window and we couldn't change seats, as the train was full. We could not afford a honeymoon – just told everyone we were spending it in London – so we went to our new flat and had meals out every evening instead.

In most cases convention still ruled that a father was responsible for the major cost of the wedding, so the reception was likely to reflect what the family could afford. Some fathers started saving for their daughter's wedding soon after she was born. For those who did not have bank accounts – and there were still many who did not – then they might take out an insurance policy, saving so much a week for a certain term of years ready for the big day.

Possibly this was what D.'s father had done, for her reception was different again. Details are sparse as to the actual event.

Ours was in a local village hall; a sit-down buffet which I believe cost six shillings a head. I found the menu and receipts when my father died. As we were Methodists, I'm not sure there was much alcohol imbibed. Dressed in a rather smart turquoise dress and coat with glorious fuchsia pink accessories and my husband in a grey suit, we went off to Alderney on honeymoon. My father was amused for the rest of his life to know that we joined the library pro-tem whilst there – not his idea of a great honeymoon, but there had not been much else to do on the island.

L.A., who lived in London, got married at noon on a Sunday and her reception took the form of 'a hot buffet lunch with roast turkey, gammon, pork and all the trimmings served by professional chefs wearing chefs' outfits. It was a great day enjoyed by all.'

R. did not return to what she had regarded as her home parish to marry. Her parents having moved to a different part of the country, her wedding took place in their new parish church. The reception was held at the newly-opened Gifford Hotel opposite the cathedral in Worcester. Asked how much it cost, R.'s reply was she couldn't remember, except that it was a lot for those days! It was a December wedding and the honeymoon was a weekend spent in London 'going round museums to keep warm'.

Just to illustrate that anything could happen in the 1960s we have this account from J.T.:

I got engaged at the end of my third year at University. It wasn't surprising that I found a husband when I lived in a Hall [of Residence] with about five hundred men! It seemed to be a natural progression after university – I wouldn't have liked to go out into the big wide world alone. It was unthinkable to live with a man unless you were married to him so we married in July 1966 in Weymouth, the day before England won the World Cup.

The marriage took place in the local church – I came down at Easter to make the arrangements and then a few days before the ceremony. I wore a very 60s style white silk wedding dress with a short train coming from the back at waist level – very plain – definitely not a meringue. I bought it from Bourne & Hollingsworth in Oxford Street for around

£35.0.0. – a month's pay was £80.0.0 at the time. I had a short lace veil. There was one bridesmaid, my husband's sister who looked stunning in a long straight style blue silk dress. We had the choir to sing the hymns (£12 extra). We had a professional photographer at the church.

We had a sit down meal for fifty at Pullinger's restaurant on the Pier Bandstand. For once I wasn't in the kitchens [J.T. had first worked there part time whilst still at school]. The fact that Mr Pullinger had once referred to me as 'Bird Brain' was raised in my father's speech. I can't remember what the wedding cost or who paid for it. I think it might have been fifteen shillings a head. My parents were not well off but I think they bore the brunt of it. The groom's family paid for the flowers as tradition dictated.

During our adult life we all tend to hang on to an odd assortment of documents quite apart from all the official ones required by law; ones that pinpoint a special moment, often in the progress of your children's life – the record card of the baby's immunisations, that first picture drawn just for you, the twenty-five yards swimming certificate, the school reports, the list is endless. But among these very personal nostalgic records there will also be bills, again marking milestones in your life, such as that for your very first three-piece suite or bedroom suite, that brand-new car as opposed to the old banger you started with, even something as simple as a receipt for a pair of rather expensive shoes. Why do we keep them? To look back and remember? Or to show our offspring and let them laugh at how little everything cost in 'the olden days'? When W. sorted through her late parents' papers she was astounded to uncover what to this author was a valuable piece of social history, in the form of the invoice from the hotel where her wedding reception was held in 1969.

Held at a country house hotel in Hertfordshire it reads as follows:

76 lunches @ 27/6	£104. 10s. 0d.
103 Sherries @ 3/6	18. 0s. 6d.
16 Entre Deux Mers @ 21/-	16. 16s. 0d.
4 Santos Rosa @ 27/6	5. 10s. 0d.
10 Raphael @ 44/6	22. 5s. 0d.
1 Jug of Fruit Cup @ 10/6	10. 6s. 6d.
	£167. 12s. 0d.
10% Staff gratuity	16. 15s. 0d.
	£184. 7s. 0d.

Room hire	3. 3s. 0d.
Flowers	5. 5s. 0d.
Changing room	2. 2s. 0d.
40 Players	12s. 2d.
40 Perfectos	<u>12s. 2d.</u>
Total	**£196. 1s. 4d.**

This was indeed a very grand affair. It was tempting to approach the hotel, which is still in existence, to ask for a comparative quote for today. Of more interest are the items which reflect life in the late Sixties, in particular the drinking habits. Sherry was of course the recognised aperitif, but quite why 103 glasses were poured out for seventy-six guests is not explained. But what a blast from the past is the mention of the white wine served with the meal. There cannot be many women from the 1960s who will not at some time or other have drunk Entre Deux Mers on a special occasion. It is interesting too, that the white wine drinkers, who possibly had their glasses topped up once during the meal, far outweighed those who opted for the more expensive red. For non-drinkers and young people there was a Fruit Cup. As for the ten bottles of Raphael at £2.4s.6d this would have been the 'bubbly' for the toasts. One other item, which reflects the Sixties, was the provision of cigarettes at the end of the meal. It was usual to have individual cigarettes placed upright in a small glass or silver container in the centre of the table alongside an ashtray and books of matches. The latter were usually printed with the name of the establishment as a form of advertisement but they could also be overprinted with the names of the bridal couple and offered as souvenirs of the occasion. It was not done to smoke during the meal on formal occasions, guests had to wait until after the loyal toast had been made and the words, 'You may now smoke' were uttered. In the 1960s cigarette-smoking was still considered acceptable by all ranks of society and it was not unusual for diners in a restaurant to smoke between courses. John Player was one of the largest manufacturers and produced several different brands, Perfectos being the one obviously aimed specifically at the male population; the cigarette itself was what became known as king size while its packaging resembled a leather case.

It is a pity that we cannot compare the price of P.T.'s reception in 1965. Like W. she was a career girl who at the age of twenty-three married a man who was still studying. Like most of the contributors she married in church and had a reception in a local hotel, hers being for eighty guests.

Coincidentally her dress sounded very similar to J.T.'s except that it was satin rather than silk, but it too had the train that came from the waist. Her veil was held in place with a small diamante coronet. She and her new husband spent their honeymoon in Majorca which must have sounded quite exotic at the time but as she noted 'that was the last holiday we could afford for several years'. P.T. showed the ingenuity and practicality of many 1960s' women when she related that shortly after the wedding her dress was dyed black and made sheath-like to wear to the University balls.

Most of the previous accounts have dealt with women who, by the time they were twenty-five, had found a husband either locally in their home town or whilst away studying. But what of those women who were in their late twenties and approaching that dreaded thirtieth birthday; in the eyes of the world about to be labelled as 'being on the shelf'? In the 1960s that prospect was every bit as mortifying as it was to poor Charlotte Lucas in Jane Austen's *Pride and Prejudice*. Mothers, who could see their chances of grandchildren disappearing, tried desperately to hide their disappointment by telling friends and relations that their daughters were going to be career women and were 'far too busy to look for a husband'. And the daughters were often happy to agree with them. After they had attended the weddings of most of their girl friends, often as bridesmaid but later just a guest, there was a lull before they were asked to take on the role of godmother to the babies that started arriving. Visiting the homes of married friends, often in uncomfortable cramped flats and hearing of their money worries, often caused the unmarried woman to appraise her own situation; she was financially better off, she was enjoying holidays they could not afford, she had a comfortable home, often shared with an ageing parent yet ... she did not have that close intimacy, the someone to share her life with, that they had.

So where did Miss Nearly Thirty find romance? The problem was probably most difficult for those who had entered the teaching profession. At that time primary schools were almost entirely staffed by women, though the head was likely to be a man, usually safely married. In the secondary sector, both grammar and secondary moderns that had not yet become comprehensives were likely to be single-sex, with the majority of their staff likewise. There was quite a flutter in the dovecote if a man was appointed to join an all-female staff. Those over fifty mothered him, the younger ones sighed when they discovered he was married with children, while it was a brave woman indeed who applied for and was appointed to an all-male staff. There she was likely to encounter even more entrenched taboos from her older colleagues than a man ever did in a female staff room. Never mind the code she had learnt in college about being careful in which chair she sat in the staff room, in case it was a certain member's particular seat; she could be ignored, have sexist remarks made about her clothes, but worst of all was to have her teaching ability questioned or even undermined in front of the pupils. Even when staff rooms did become mixed, there were very few romances that resulted in first-time marriages.

A school staff room might not be the most likely place for romance but other workplaces were more productive. One woman who swapped teaching maths for working with computers found that love blossomed for her there. A rather shy woman who apparently had no interest in a social life that involved such activities as dancing or visiting places where men abounded, she found herself working alongside a young man who was as retiring as she was. They discovered they had similar interests in opera, ballet and classical music concerts. It was not long before an invitation to use one of the two tickets he had purchased for a Saturday evening musical treat led to a regular meal for two, either before or after a performance, and before their friends knew what had happened they were engaged to be married.

Working alongside a male colleague and developing a friendship with him was quite different from being put in a possibly romantic situation. For example, the kind-hearted friends who thought they were doing a single woman a good turn by inviting her to a supper party where among the other guests at the table was the only unattached man. This was such obvious matchmaking that it instantly put a restraint on both of them. At least that was not quite so awful as going on a blind date with a couple who were totally wrapped up in each other. The usual reaction here was to be polite to each other but to curtail the 'date' as quickly as possible. It has to be admitted however that sometimes tagging along with your best friend could work, indeed one couple who met like this have now celebrated their diamond wedding.

Other 'late developers' could find themselves inadvertently caught up in workplace romances. Considering the length of the working day, it was not surprising that working in close proximity, people came to know each other really well and that in some cases romance might develop. This was fine if both parties were single, but all too often the man in question was married with a family. The attraction was understandable; the woman he worked with was bright and intelligent, she dressed well and took care of her looks. She would leave the office after work perhaps for an evening at the theatre or out to dinner while he went home to a wife and young family; to a wife who was too tired to heed the words of the romantic novelist Barbara Cartland to bathe and dress herself for her husband's homecoming before serving up the delicious dinner she had made specially for him. No, his wife was probably in the clothes she had worn all day as she coped with the tantrums of a two-year-old and a teething baby, along with all the other routine chores. She was as likely to greet him at the sound of his key in the lock not with a lingering kiss but with a list of things that had gone wrong and that he needed to sort out. His female colleague would hear all about this the next day and would offer her sympathy. If she was sensible she might have sympathy with the wife too and even offer to babysit so that the couple could have an evening out together. On the other hand, heart might rule head, and the working relationship would become an affair.

The 1960s social scene brought with it a much more relaxed attitude between the sexes partly influenced by the fact that higher education and job opportunities had been responsible for a shift in the population. Where previously people tended to grow up, find work and eventually settle down and marry someone from within their community, now they were scattered far away from parental influences – and their moral standards. In a close-knit locality, if a married man or woman was seen visiting or out with someone who was not their spouse, then gossip or even straight talking from a family member would be brought to bear upon them. But in a large town or city where one was relatively unknown except to a small group of people, then one could take advantage of flirting at a supper party, or going for a drink with your badminton or tennis partner after a match, innocent activities in themselves, yet both could, and often did, lead to dangerous consequences. For the upwardly-mobile employees of large firms and industries, their formal dinner dances and Christmas parties gave them ample opportunity to dance perhaps slightly closer than they should have done and the kiss under the mistletoe could become more than a peck on the cheek or a simple brush of the lips. All too often these parties, especially when too much alcohol was consumed, led to dire consequences. They could result in a marriage breakdown or more often, the single woman who was by then besotted with the married colleague found herself becoming 'the other woman'.

This was a wholly unsatisfactory position to be in, yet many unmarried women accepted the surreptitious meetings after work knowing full well that they could never have anything more and that even that could be cancelled if the man's family commitments demanded. Sadly, there were some very naïve women who not only accepted this, they lived in a dream world. They did not succumb to a sexual relationship with the man, being content with the odd embrace and kiss, but as long as they could be in the same room with him, even with others present, they were happy. They liked to make themselves useful to him, running errands for him, even buying his clothes for him – one even spent Christmas with him and his wife and children. This woman, who seemed to come alive when she was near him and talked freely about him to her family without, so she thought, betraying her true feelings for him, believed that he loved her as much as she loved him. When he ultimately betrayed her, and more importantly his wife, by running off with a younger woman, she remained faithful to his memory to her dying day.

Another woman in her mid-twenties who fell in love with a work colleague realised she was flouting custom by setting up home with him. She knew he was married but he had left his wife whom he hoped would eventually divorce him for desertion, at that time one of the recognised requirements for a divorce. The couple lived very happily together, although to avoid scandal and tongues wagging they had both left their original employment and moved to an area where neither was known. One Friday evening she got home first as usual and started making their evening meal. Uncharacteristically her partner was late. Time passed and still he had not arrived. Remember, this was the era before few people, especially those who lived in a flat in a multi-occupancy house had access to a telephone and long before mobile phones were invented. As the evening wore on there was still no sign of him and so she waited, frantic with worry. What should she do? What could she do? As they had deliberately cut themselves off from previous acquaintances, she had no idea who to contact. Throughout the long night she imagined different scenarios, the most obvious being that perhaps he had left her. After all, he had left his wife, was history repeating itself? It was three or four days later that she received a terse note from his brother telling her he would call to collect the man's belongings and that he had been killed in a road accident. As his legal next of kin, the police had informed his wife of his death. Shocked, alone with no one close to confide in or comfort her on her great loss, worse was to follow when the brother, carrying out his mission, told her in no uncertain terms that she must on no account attempt to attend her lover's funeral. She had no rights.

It was not, however, always a single woman who embarked on an affair with a work colleague. A married woman was just as likely to be tempted, especially if she was finding her own marriage becoming stale for one reason or another. We tend to hear of cases of young unmarried girls becoming pregnant and the awful upheaval that caused but there were also casualties among married women. The likelihood was that their lover would try to persuade them to have an illegal abortion and if they refused, the women would then face rejection by the lover, possibly loss of employment, as well as having to confess to the husband. Some women tried to brazen it out making their husband believe that the child was his. In some cases this worked, in others where the wife had been truthful, although the man accepted the child, it was a constant reminder of the wife's infidelity and later, the child itself became aware that for some reason her father did not love her as much as her siblings. Depending on the background of the couple concerned, a divorce might be the only way out of the situation.

Statistics tell us that while marriages peaked in the 1960s, the increase in the divorce rate from the previous decade continued to rise also. Although the Royal Commission on Divorce in the 1950s had recognised that times and attitudes to marriage had changed it was still necessary to prove that the marriage had broken down because of adultery by one of the partners, cruelty, or desertion for at least three years. In the mid-Sixties, the question of the breakdown of marriage was looked at under the auspices of the then Archbishop of Canterbury but it was to be the very end of the decade before the new measures were enacted. Until then many couples were locked into loveless, incompatible or damaged marriages. Divorce, like sex before marriage, was still regarded by many as being shameful, bringing disgrace on the family name and humiliation in front of the neighbours. Many wives were encouraged by their parents to stay with an adulterous or abusive husband rather than making a clean break. Financial considerations weighed heavily against a woman with children even to think of leaving a marriage. Unless she had a good job sufficient to provide a home and pay all their living costs including child care, or had ultra-sympathetic parents, then she was stuck. However, we must not forget that women could also be what was termed the guilty party; those who were divorced by their husbands and went on to marry the man with whom they had had an affair sometimes found they were disowned by their families.

So it was that during the 1960s that divorce provided a new pool of men available to those women who had previously found difficulty in finding a suitable husband. However, it still raised the question of how was Miss Nearly Thirty going to meet one of this new breed. Of course, there was always that good old fall-back recommended by all the Agony Aunts in their magazine columns, Evening Classes. In the past, men had eschewed those classes traditionally taken by women, but perhaps, now that they were living on their own, they might be found attending cookery classes? The other standard suggestion was to join in activities in one's local church but, given the attitude that still existed on the subject of divorce, this did not seem to be the most obvious of hunting grounds either. So where else? There had been a time when public houses were regarded as male preserves; wives and steady girlfriends were tolerated in the lounge bar but unless she wished to be thought of as looking for custom, it was a brave woman who ventured on her own into a pub. But come the Sixties, things were changing here too. Two young women out for an evening might choose to sit in the warmth of a lounge bar with a glass of Babycham or a gin and orange and catch up with each other's news as they smoked a cigarette or two. P.H., a college lecturer, commented on this:

> I started smoking in the Sixties, which did have a huge impact on my life since it was 1974 before I managed to give up. I did not start because I wanted to but because it was the socially acceptable thing to do. This was the decade when I started going into pubs, something I wouldn't have dared to do before. At the beginning of the 1960s it really wasn't the thing for a lady to enter a pub alone, but by 1967 I was happily going into my local without an escort. I met my husband there, so I suppose that had more impact on my life than smoking!

The other option open to women looking for a partner is one that has become widely used nowadays but in the 1960s was considered either very daring or rather sad. It was in the spring of 1939 that The Marriage Bureau opened in Bond Street in the heart of London's Mayfair. Heather Jenner, herself newly divorced, and a friend had recognised the problem that some people who wanted to settle down to married life had in meeting a suitable partner. It was aimed mainly at men who were either too busy in their careers to attend social functions where they might meet someone or, in particular, those working abroad, often for the government, who again did not have the opportunity to meet a suitable wife. These men usually came home for a possible two or three months' leave every two years. It was hard for them, even with help from friends, to be introduced to a girl who would be willing not just to marry them after a short courtship but also commit to living in another country. The Marriage Bureau advertised discreetly in the broadsheet newspapers and ladies' magazines. Clients were interviewed and carefully questioned, fees were paid and in due course, suitable couples were introduced by letter. Such was the ethos of the period that the woman who used the name Heather Jenner did not admit to her own family what business she had entered. But she had discovered there was a great the need for such a service and during those first few months the bureau was swamped with requests for introductions. After the war, other bureaux opened throughout the country and more newspapers began to operate 'lonely hearts' columns. Two young women recall the fun they had on those Saturday evenings at the beginning of the 1960s when they had neither a party nor dance to attend. Instead they would settle themselves down to select suitable applicants from the columns of *Daltons Weekly*; they laughed a lot as they did so but would never have dared answer an advertiser. More serious were the advertisements which appeared in the *Farmers Weekly*. Busy agriculturists had little time to spare for social activities beyond, perhaps, Young Farmers Clubs and these did not always produce young women who were looking to become farmers' wives. On the other hand there were lonely young women who hankered for a life in the country and all that would entail.

During the 1960s, more and more men and women were availing themselves of the services of a marriage bureau, although they were often reluctant to admit it. Many women felt that to do so would mark them down as being too unattractive to find a partner within the circles in which they moved. It could also, they reasoned, be taken by others as a sign of desperation. So they went about their applications and eventual meetings with a selected partner surreptitiously, however hard they tried to tell themselves that what they were doing was sensible. Unlike casual meetings, both parties had declared that they wished to find a partner for life and in most cases, after corresponding with each other for some time, they were able to meet finally as friends knowing a great deal about each other. This was particularly useful for the man living abroad who, knowing he would be back in the United Kingdom within, say, the following six months, was able to establish the preliminaries of a courtship by letters. There were, naturally, a few false starts in introductions, but eventually there was a meeting of minds and love finally blossomed. It is very different now with online dating, speed dating and parties set up specifically for dating purposes. Nowadays, no one turns a hair if a woman says she met her husband online. The biggest difference in this electronic age is that neither party now has that precious collection of letters that accompanied their love affair.

Longevity in marriage is reassuring, yet not to be taken for granted. If this were an analytical survey of the conduct of the contributors, would we be surprised at how many of those marriages, which got off to such a good start actually ended in divorce? If we were psychic, could we predict which couples would not stay together? We might make assumptions about the very young couples who were rushed into marriages because there was a baby on the way. Surely, at eighteen or just under, they were too young, they had not grown up, they did not know what they really wanted from life, one can almost hear the dire warnings of those onlookers at the hastily arranged weddings, yet, of all those particular cases mentioned here, all the marriages survived. It would seem the couples grew up together and gained strength from each other, learning the hard way that it requires effort to make a marriage work. The surprise was to discover that several of the marriages of the young women who had met their partners at university had failed by the 1970s and that the women had gone to remarry not once but twice before they found true compatibility. For the onlooker looking at M.O.'s account for example, it hardly came as a surprise to learn that she would divorce her husband. Their relationship highlighted the difference between men and women's attitude to life during the 1960s. By his own standards, M.O.'s husband was a good example of what a husband should be; he worked hard to provide for his family, believing that it was his place to do so. He knew his place and he expected his wife to know hers – which was in the home, looking after him and the children just as his mother had done, He liked things to be normal and could not understand that his wife, who had worked hard to achieve a good position in an office before marriage, should not be content to give it all up and behave just like the wives of his friends. The phrase 'none of his friends' wives did … ' whatever it was M.O. wanted to do, like learning to drive, echoed throughout her account. M.O., like many of the women of her generation wanted what was best for her children as well as for herself. She was not content to be the compliant housewife, she had a brain and talent and the opportunities to use them were there for the grasping - and grasp them she did. Happily, she also eventually married a man who appreciated her as a person rather than a housekeeper.

While very slowly some men were changing their idea of what marriage meant and, if their wives were working, were even taking their share of domestic chores, we still had a very long way to go to reach today's domestic set-ups. Married women in the 1960s were still often regarded in relation to their husband's position in life. Even Dr A., herself a successful single woman, described her former part-time colleague as 'the Police Inspector's wife' in her recent memoir. Many young career women were irked at being introduced at social functions as 'So and So's wife', feeling that this somehow demeaned what they did. But as married women they were considered their husbands' responsibility, unable to make financial or legal decisions without their consent. The working wife's salary could not be considered when a couple applied for a mortgage, for example: neither would her employment be taken into account should her husband be given promotion that involved moving to another area. Many young career women were faced with having to give up the job that they had trained for and enjoyed to accompany their husband on his career journey. No doubt if the Police Inspector was promoted to another area, his doctor wife would have been expected to accompany him; it was taken for granted she would want to go – it was her duty. The doctor concerned would probably be able to find another practice crying out for her services but she was one of the lucky ones. Decisions such as these must have put a strain on relationships which were perhaps already shaky and could lead to eventual divorce.

Chapter Four

Homes

The late 1950s saw a frenzy in house-building. The post-war period had revealed a double problem; an acute shortage of houses as a result of bomb damage and the rising demand for homes for all the young married couples. Progress was slow to start with due to shortages of building materials, particularly those that were imported. After 1945, one way to deal with the problem was to build estates of prefabricated single-storey houses. These, which came fully fitted with modern, dream kitchens and bathrooms, even a form of central heating, would last, it was believed, about twenty to twenty-five years. The fact, that many are still in existence, often because they are so beloved by their tenants, is amazing. Even more amazing was an item which appeared on a TV news programme in August 2014 that one English council had resorted to easing the local demand for housing by buying-in prefabricated two-bedroom units that could be ready for occupation within two weeks.

The mention of the local council highlights the responsibility that was laid down between the wars upon the borough and district councils to provide homes at an affordable rent for those who needed it. As mentioned earlier, it was customary for most people in Britain to rent their house from private landlords who invested their capital in houses. Matters changed slightly between the two World Wars when groups of potential house-owners formed Freehold Societies which enabled them to buy land and build houses for sale to members. This in turn led to the formation of local Building Societies funded by investors and small savers, which were able to lend to potential buyers. However, by the outbreak of the Second World War in 1939 home ownership was still rare. The change came in the Fifties and Sixties when local authorities were stretched to the limit building as many large, well laid-out estates as they could, so the field was clear for others to step in to try to fill the gap. It would appear that there were few individuals with sufficient money to invest to finance a small project so it fell to the large building firms as well as smaller local builders to buy up land and then build speculatively, not for rent, but for sale. They may have appeared to be taking a risk but the demand was there.

Although there was a popular slogan of 'homes for all', many 1960s women started their married life in so-called flats, usually a bedroom and living room with a share in the kitchen and bathroom, in someone else's house. With the right landlord/lady this could prove reasonably satisfactory but in a large house with multi-occupancy life was not so easy. The oft-repeated television sitcom *Rising Damp* was not far from reality, particularly in London and most large towns, where once gracious Victorian three- and four-storey houses were turned into what were euphemistically called 'flats'. Here, spacious rooms were divided in two to provide a living room and bedroom. As many 'flats' were carved out as was possible but there was one huge drawback, the water supply. The living room might be equipped with either a gas ring or small electric cooker but it was unlikely to have a sink with a cold tap. So water would have to be fetched from the bathroom of which there was likely to be just the one in the whole house. Heating the water for a bath was done by what J.T. has described elsewhere as an 'exploding gas geyser'. Extortionate rents were frequently charged for this accommodation, which offered little beyond a roof over the tenant's head. One abiding memory of this type of multi-occupied house was the timed lighting system on the staircases. One pressed the switch at the bottom of the stairs but the light had the habit of going out before one reached the first landing where the next switch was situated. Should you be unfortunate enough to occupy rooms in the attic, you took your life in your hands as there was no natural light on the stairs up there. Another memory was the smell – mainly of stale cooking. One wonders how people put up with such conditions but they did.

With the waiting list for council houses showing no sign of shortening, many young couples began to consider seriously the possibility of actually buying their own home rather than renting for life as their parents did. If a newly-married woman carried on working, then the couple could save towards the down-payment on a house – provided they were able to secure a mortgage. That was not to be taken for granted.

Early in 1960 I was engaged to P and busy house hunting with a June wedding and a honeymoon in Jersey planned. House hunting was a real problem. We had been saving for two years and had enough money for a house but not for the expenses involved. We spent a bad Sunday afternoon waiting to see someone at a new development only to be told quite bluntly that we could not afford to buy even a small house. Peter did not earn enough – his basic pay was not good, he had to work overtime to bring it up to a decent rate. I was earning good money, probably more than Peter on an hourly basis – but the Building Society would not take this into account.

M.O., whom we have already met, and P. eventually bought a plot of land directly from a builder who then built them a small bungalow for which they did get a mortgage, but paying that left them with very little to buy furniture and essential items. Another couple, G. and her fiancé also had difficulties securing a mortgage. Her future husband was a L/Sgt in the 1st Battalion of the Grenadier Guards and they married just after he was demobbed in 1961.They had applied for a mortgage on a very old terrace house but while on their honeymoon they heard that it had been refused. For the next six months they lived with her in-laws.

> The parents' house was very old fashioned. Outside toilet – there was no bathroom. Bath taken once a week in a galvanised large bath [usually kept hung] on a hook on the garden fence. Hot water had to be heated in the corner copper [in the kitchen] and transferred to the bath.
>   March 1962 – paid a deposit on an old semi-detached house in town. (The parents thought this unnecessary, as they had always rented.) [We had] very little furniture; a bed but no bedroom suite, no stair carpet, fridge, freezer, washing machine or central heating. I worked full time. In the dreadful freezing winter of 1963 our underground pipes froze and we were without running water for three weeks. Our kindly next-door neighbours allowed us to fill up a few buckets of water each day. Our meagre coal fire (lit only in the evenings) was quite inadequate in heating our cold sitting room and the rest of the house. [The following year] our home was considered unsuitable for a home birth. There was a bathroom upstairs with a cranky, noisy old gas geyser for hot water (thought the whole place would explode when it lit up) but no toilet. The toilet was downstairs; an extension attached to the kitchen.

In September 1964 G. and her husband reserved a plot for a modest new semi-detached house but they had to wait six months for its completion. The house was finished but the roads and paths were still unmade on that very rainy day in March 1965 when the family moved in to what G. described as 'a decent modern home'.

> Our new home had a Raeburn back boiler fitted to the fire in the lounge and two small radiators. The fire had to be banked-up really high at night. It had an extremely large ashtray beneath it and all the ash had to be riddled through into it. It was horrendous to empty when there were high winds. The bathroom had an electric wall heater placed close to the ceiling with a pull switch. In October of that year our son was born. He was born at home but things might have been easier if he had been born in hospital. The 'flying squad' was called in to help me. The afterbirth had to be manually removed. I received two pints of blood. The doctor had to hold up the bags of blood, as they did not like to knock a hole into a cupboard, as the house was new. My husband, although worried, was annoyed with me that so many men saw me in a state of undress! He was looking after our young daughter and the midwife was amazed later when she saw him hoovering.

This short account illustrates several aspects of the slow changes that were taking place in the 1960s, the first being the introduction of a limited form of central heating which was dependent on the old-established coal fire in the family living room. The back boiler provided hot water to both the kitchen and the bathroom so that was the end of the 'exploding geysers'. Once there was hot water on tap and an indoor lavatory, then a house was deemed suitable for a home birth, as it was for G. This being her second child, the midwife was not anticipating any trouble. It was a tribute to the National Health Service that help was readily available. Had G. lived in a rural area it might have been a very different story. At this distance in time, it is possible to have a little smile at the picture of the doctor being reluctant to have nails hammered into a new cupboard to support the transfusion equipment. As for G.'s husband he represents the old and new man – the one appalled at the invasion of his wife's modesty, the other happily looking after his other child and doing domestic chores.

It is interesting that in describing the first house they bought, G. used the term 'sitting room', for it was in the Sixties that not only did house designs change but so too did terminology to describe their interior layout. For generations the most common design for a town house, whether it were detached, semi-detached or part of a terrace, was based on rooms stretching from front to back on the plot. This harked back to the days when the rateable valuable of a house was assessed on how much space it occupied at street level. Thus the façade contained one window and a front door on the ground floor with a window to match the one below and possibly another above the door on the next floor. Depending on the size of the house there may or not have been an entrance hall. Behind the front room, variously known as the parlour or sitting room – or even simply the front room – was the dining room or family living room. These two rooms were usually of similar size, unless the house did not have a hall in which case the stairs went out of this room, usually hidden behind a wall and accessed by what looked like a cupboard door. The much smaller kitchen often gave the impression that it had been added as an afterthought. Sometimes adjoining buildings housed the outside lavatory and coal shed. Again, depending on the size of the building, it stretched out into either a small backyard or a fair-sized garden.

That all changed in the Fifties when architects drawing up plans for the new estates hit on the idea of giving the illusion of more space for each house and so we go from the elongated house to the rectangular one. In this design there was still a front room and a back room but the kitchen has now got bigger and leads off the dining room which has in turn got smaller. It had long been an accepted fact – and in some cases a standing joke – that the front room was little used by a large majority of the population. It was the room that contained a three-piece suite, a china display cabinet, dated pictures on the walls and in many houses, a piano. It was used mainly at Christmas time, for special occasions and funerals. Apart from preserving the best furniture, its infrequent use was because it was usually a very cold room. In those pre-central heating days, to use it meant lighting another fire in addition to the one in the family living room or adding to the electricity bill by switching on the one-bar electric fire which always emitted a very dusty smell as the element slowly warmed up. Ask any woman who was a child in the 1950s and early 1960s and they will still shudder as they recall being forced into that icebox of a front room to perform the regulation half-hour piano practice.

By the Sixties the emphasis was on making use of all available space and making it as light and airy as possible. So the first move was to remove the wall between sitting room and dining room, replacing it with double glass doors and adding French windows in the latter. The next step was towards even more open-plan living, getting rid of the idea of separate rooms and creating the L-shaped living room. It was at this point that estate agents, presumably, adopted the word 'lounge' to describe this new layout. To most people at the time the word had connotations with either a hotel or the bar in a public house considered suitable for women. Further innovations included dispensing with wooden floorboards and covering the whole of the ground floor area with vinyl tiles on a concrete base. If one managed to buy a house before it was completed, then it was often possible to have a say in the colour and design of tiles. For the new homeowner who could not afford rugs, this seemingly vast area of blue and grey with a hint of black tiles was, to say the least, difficult to keep clean, especially when they first moved in and both the garden and the road outside, were still unmade.

Although many couples were forced into home ownership because of the lack of rented housing, there were areas of the country where it was still possible to rent a new-build as J.T. and her husband, who married in 1966, found when they moved to a new town.

We had a fabulous new experimental architect designed house in an area in Harlow that appealed to young professionals.[1] Everyday busloads of foreign architectural students would roll up just to see the place known locally as the 'Casbah'! In the mid-1960s many people took up the £10 ticket to Australia and they only got two weeks' notice of their sailing date. Their 'Contents of home for sale' notices in the local paper were a godsend for young people like us needing to furnish our new home. Apart from the new gas cooker we bought on hire purchase from the Gas Board everything else came from the emigrants.

Later, when we had been earning for a while, we were able to buy the new stylish 1960s home furnishings. First was a wonderful G Plan sleek long line teak dressing table, then a G Plan Fresco sideboard and coffee table. Small items came from Habitat and we bought a fantastic turquoise and purple Scandinavian large rug from Heals in Tottenham Court Road in London. This was for our mezzanine lounge which

---

1. Readers who would like to know more about the winning architect-designed house – and see J.T. herself sitting in the mezzanine lounge – can go to http:// www.eafa.org.uk/ catalogue/253 East Anglia Film Archive - A View of Bishopsfield 1969 Harlow, Essex. When asked in 2014, J.T. was unable to provide any relevant photographs but her search of the Internet revealed this film. She has no recollection of the filming but the sight of the young woman's dress made her realise she was looking at her much younger self!

overlooked the large kitchen, dining room and faced a twenty feet high wall of glass.

J.T.'s family and friends who lived in run-of-the mill houses must have marvelled when they saw where she was living, especially with its mezzanine floor. The design was adapted and scaled down later for use as split-level houses on sloping sites. It was also in the Sixties that some more daring builders actually took account of the location of the building plot and, where the view warranted it, placed sitting rooms on the first floor, stretching the whole width of the front of the house, with three bedrooms and the bathroom occupying the back half. Downstairs contained the dining room, a large kitchen and – this was something new – a utility room, for the washing machine, tumble dryer and possibly a chest freezer. There would also be a downstairs cloakroom and a small room known as the study. These houses were not for everyone – they belonged to the families of men who had been promoted to the managerial class but they were something to aspire to and they set the pattern for the future. As too did the designs for individually built houses – and particularly bungalows that appeared in the *Daily Mail* Ideal Home's Plan-a-Homes books. Many young couples must have spent hours leafing through the black-and-white sketches of 'dream' homes. Stone rather than brick featured strongly in these with their wide arch covered front porches and their novel stoneclad chimneys into which were incorporated an outdoor barbecue. Some designers, while playing about with the layout of a house, decided to locate the kitchen at the front of the house facing the road. The thinking behind this move was that it allowed the living area to take advantage of the view of the garden. While some housewives may have welcomed the opportunity to watch their neighbours come and go while they were standing at the kitchen sink, the biggest drawback for mothers was that they could no longer keep an eye on small children playing in the garden. A further consideration was that unless the kitchen had direct access to the garden from the side of the house, then laundry and rubbish had to be carried through the house.

Then there were the wooden kit houses which looked so well when placed in natural surroundings. In stark contrast to these were the high-rise blocks of flats built mainly by local authorities to deal with the shortage of homes in towns and cities. Many became blots on the landscape, particularly those built when grey cement was the architects' favoured building material. But what excuse could be found for the speculative builders who produced an estate of monstrosities; rows of small detached bungalows which had the front door on one side of the building and the back door immediately opposite on the other side. On one such site visited before they were completed it was possible to enter house number one and then, walking in a straight line go through the whole row of fifty houses. Malvina Reynolds's 1962 song 'Little Boxes' made famous by Pete Seager the following year could not have been more apt, these really were made of 'ticky tacky'.

Few couples, once they had secured a house, could afford to furnish it straight away. Many started with little more than a bed, a table and a couple of chairs. Friends and relations passed on unwanted pieces such as an old dressing table or wardrobe or the couples scoured second-hand shops and 'For sale' advertisements in shop windows or the local newspaper. Not many were able to pick up the bargains mentioned by J.T. Second-hand furniture generally meant late Victorian or Edwardian pieces that were regarded in the Sixties as being highly unfashionable. No one wanted the heavy old mahogany bedroom suites for instance, especially the now-defunct washstand with its marble top and marble or tiled splashback. The canny couple could get one of these for a couple of pounds and having removed the marble – often just discarding it, and replacing it with a piece of wood – and the whole item painted, then they had a perfectly serviceable sideboard until they could afford to buy new and modern. An oak oval gate-legged folding table that had once graced a dining room or perhaps a drawing room, rejected as antiquated by its owner fifty years ago, was picked up for £3 in 1965 and has been in use ever since.

Those setting-up home in the 1960s had been brought up by their parents that 'money did not grow on trees' and that it was necessary to save in order to buy. Most people, however, had accepted that it was permissible to purchase a gas or electric oven on hire purchase from their local gas or electricity showroom where the repayment instalments were added to one's bill. But in general the older generation looked askance at hire purchase schemes. Memories and old family stories were still related of people getting into serious debt with moneylenders or having to pawn Sunday-best clothes on Monday in order to put food on the table or buy a pair of shoes for a child, in the hope that by Saturday, Friday's pay packet could be used to redeem the clothes. Although young people in the Sixties had more disposable income than their parents had had, they also had far more tempting items vying to be bought. J.T. mentions in her account that all her original furnishings were bought cheaply from the emigrants but as she and her husband earned more they bought new. Notice that she said 'First was a ...': in other words, they bought when they had saved enough to pay for an item. Unless they had been given very generous wedding presents such as a bedroom suite or dining suite, most women decided what they needed most and then bought piecemeal, adding to it when they could. And what enjoyment they got out of each new acquisition.

The names G Plan and Ercol occur over and over again in the reminiscences of the Sixties women. The furniture from these two old-established firms said both quality and modern style. The sleek lines of teak dining-room suites and the soft warm glow of beech and ash added to the light airy feel of modern interiors. Out went the heavy suites covered in uncut moquette that had graced the front rooms of our parents' generation. In came the useful, lightly padded material covered settees with a back that could fold down to make a guest bed and the curved wooden sofas and armchairs with their loosely-tied cushions. These were the epitome of style and in addition they were light enough to be movable to anywhere in the room and with their uncluttered legs they allowed for easy cleaning. The move to leave space at floor level resulted in another furniture trend which has now been passed over and that was the use of ladders to form storage units. Teak shelves of different sizes had clips at each end that either slotted into or hooked over the ladder rung. The joy of this system is that one could add as many ladders or shelves as one wanted, or could afford. The shelves could house books, ornaments, radios, record players, whatever one wanted. There was no doubt that for many people teak was the favoured wood of the Sixties.

For the artistic and the more daring, 1960s designs offered a whole new range of exciting concepts. Following her marriage in 1968, W. found herself living in a village outside Swansea in a new build end-on chalet bungalow. 'Downstairs it had a sizeable kitchen, a small ancillary room and a wide sitting room, with a low picture window and view to the Carmarthen Hills. Upstairs there was a bathroom and two bedrooms. It cost £3,570.' While still at work and the house not yet completed, W. had given much thought to the interior decoration.

I ordered from John Lewis a remarkable bed settee. It was effectively a single mattress supported by steel mesh on a white tubular steel frame. There were low, buttoned triangular profile arms/bed-ends and the back flipped down to expose the full mattress area. Apart from the underside of the mattress/seat which was in ticking, the whole was upholstered in muted grey, mustard, olive green and wine coloured William Morris 'Vine'. I decided on a 'Thames Green' carpet, and curtains in wide stripes of beige, mauve and charcoal hessian from Heals. The uncarpeted bedroom had a black goatskin rug and curtains of magenta slubbed cotton. The bathroom curtain material was also from heals The uncompromising cotton print is in turquoise, kingfisher, purple, mauve, navy blue and olive green semi circles and stripes. It is a classic 60s design.

From John Lewis in Oxford Street I bought a plain square whitewood table for 79/6d [almost £4 0s 0d.] which I painted white with the new polyurethane paint. It repaid the repeated sanding between coats with a fine satin surface. I also bought a table and four bentwood chairs from Habitat in Tottenham Court Road.

W.'s descriptions of her interior decoration and J.T.'s reference to a turquoise and purple rug will no doubt revive memories of the brilliant colours in use during the period. Orange seemed to predominate, especially when teamed with brown. Bold colours too dominated in carpets; greens, orange, yellows in abstract swirls or geometric patterns covered stairs and halls as well as living rooms. Linoleum had long been ripped from floors to be replaced with sheets of vinyl in the same dazzling bright colours and designs. Walls were covered with bold patterned wallpaper; sometimes two different papers were placed on the walls in the same room or three walls were painted and the fourth papered. B recalled; 'our first home needed lots of TLC, decorating and DIY. I remember our lounge wallpaper was a heavy all–over trellis pattern. Tangerine was a popular colour and ghastly! Mushroom too.' Gone from the Sixties' house were picture rails, dados and in some cases skirting boards, leaving walls uncluttered. There was also a craze for putting in false ceilings. DYI had really come into its own and women led the way with home improvements, making suggestions and then carrying them out themselves if their husbands were reluctant to do the job.

Colour had come to the rest of the house too. The pale green, yellow or blue of the standard sink units and cupboards in the kitchen had given way to brightly-coloured Formica worktops and cupboard fronts. Out too went the deep white sinks and wooden draining boards to be replaced by a single unit in stainless steel. Most kitchens were equipped in similar fashion; the sink unit with its double cupboard, one side to hide the water and waste pipes, the other to house the plastic bucket and washing-up bowl and household cleaning materials. The sink was invariable placed under the window and a space was left next to it for a washing machine. This was essential as many of the machines emptied the used water via a hosepipe into the sink. Depending on the size of the kitchen the oven could be placed beside the end of the draining board. The moulded stainless steel sinks tended to come with only one draining board, so for anyone replacing an old sink there could be a choice of having either a right- or left-hand drainer. How many 1960s women must have dreamed of one day owning a dishwasher, especially at Christmas or other occasions when large numbers were catered for. But such a piece of equipment was a real luxury; there were other kitchen items that were higher on the list of essentials. Where the 1950s housewife had had a mass-produced unit that consisted of a double cupboard below with above it a pull-down enamel topped flap that served as a work top when cooking with above that a couple of glass-fronted cupboards for storage of tins and dry goods, by the Sixties there was a demand for more cupboard space, especially as new houses no longer had larders. Reasonably-priced wall cupboards in whitewood could be bought for the kitchen that came with nothing more than the sink unit. Initially these consisted of an open shelf above with a small (in height) cupboard below with sliding doors. These cupboards seemed designed to take only tins and packets of a standard size. Matching floor units, such as broom and larder cupboards, could be added as when one could afford them. Then it was up to the owners to paint them to suit their own taste. For tips and guidance on how to achieve the best effect, 1960s women were given valuable assistance by their favourite women's magazines.

As the decade progressed, not only did the kitchen become more sophisticated but so did much else in the house. Hot water on tap, which was unheard of in many older houses even in the post-war years, had now become a reality where it was possible to install a water tank that could be heated by an electric immersion heater. Once this was installed it was goodbye to the fearsome geyser or the more modern gas water heater over the bath. The drawback to the immersion heater was the length of time it took to reheat the tank once someone had drawn off enough for a bath. Other means of heating water that would provide hot water to service radiators throughout the house, as had existed for years in the homes of the very wealthy, depended on solid fuel boilers. Small versions of coke boilers were installed in many new houses in the Sixties often replacing the back boilers which had been fitted to the living-room fire. With an emphasis on the use of smokeless fuel and rising coal prices, plus a reluctance of women to spend time on making and clearing fires, the trend was to do away with fires altogether.

Many houses were even built without fireplaces, with electric fires inserted into a focal point in the living room or gas fires were inserted into grates and old-fashioned surrounds were stripped out to be replaced with features – of wood or stone – that might incorporate shelves for ornaments or a music system. For Christmas the first year of their marriage, S.M. and her husband gave each other the very latest in gas fires!

There were other forms of central heating apart from radiators including the rather cumbersome and somewhat temperamental electric storage heaters. Then there was underfloor warm air heating which would waft the air through ducts around the house. S.M.'s second house, which had been built to the design of the Ideal Home 'House of the Year' in the mid-1960s, was equipped with this form of heating. No protruding radiators taking up valuable wall space, only strategically-placed grilles, just above skirting- , board level, through which the warm air escaped.

It was particularly chilly one autumn afternoon, so I turned on the heating before I lay down on the settee for the rest I was supposed to take as I was pregnant. I settled down to listen to the Saturday play on the radio, the setting for which was a small ship carrying a cargo of rice from China. Violent storms overtook the ship and the flooding in the hold caused the ship to founder. I remember thinking how good the sound effects of gushing water were. The play ended, but the sound of rushing water continued. My first thought was that a pipe had burst somewhere in the house but after investigation I realised the water was coming from the trunking behind the walls. I was on my own, my husband was away on business, so what to do? Eventually I phoned the local builder who had built the house and explained the situation. From the tone of his voice it was quite obvious that he thought I was imagining it. You could almost hear him thinking I was being hysterical because of my condition. However, he did come and to his horror he discovered there was indeed at least an inch of water in the duct … Several days later when a sort of ditch had been excavated all around the house it was discovered that the house had been built on a very high water table. 'But of course' said one of my neighbours, 'in the old days there was a pond on this spot!'

For those who had grown up in houses with indoor bathrooms – and there were still plenty without such a facility – this room tended to be rather bleak normally and very cold in winter. The room, which could be quite small, was dominated by a large cast-iron bath which itself was very cold to the touch and tended to cool down the water as it filled. The atmosphere was certainly not conducive to creating a desire to strip off and linger in the hot water when you knew you had to get out, stepping perhaps on a flimsy mat covering the cold lino and then drying in the cold air. What was needed was a bathroom heater. Some people used paraffin heaters to warm the room in advance. One poor unfortunate teacher, having hurriedly arranged accommodation close to the school she was joining, had seen the bedsitter with its adjoining kitchen but had not thought to ask about the bathroom. Imagine her horror when, having unpacked her suitcase, she discovered that both lavatory and bathroom were outside! She learned to live with the situation for a year mainly because her amenable landlady did her best. They would discuss which nights they would have their baths; the landlady would go home at lunchtime to turn on the water heater and in winter she would light the paraffin stove. The landlady had the first bath, so by the time it was the teacher's turn, the little outhouse had become thoroughly warm. But there was still the trek from house to bathroom and back to be made wearing an overcoat over dressing gown and, in the depth of winter, complete with boots!

Before radiators could be extended to bathrooms or heated towel rails became a possibility, the two main ways of heating the area were either by a heat-emitting ring plugged into the electric light socket or a small electric fire placed high up on the wall opposite the bath which was switched on and off by a string pull located outside the bathroom door. Actually many bathrooms in newly-built houses were so small that heating was not necessary. And the builders were no longer installing the old-fashioned heavy cast-iron baths replacing them with the softer, and warmer to the touch, vinyl moulded baths which could be mass produced cheaply. Once these were introduced then out too, went the porcelain washbasins to be replaced by vinyl bowls which did not need dust-collecting pedestals to support them. Any unsightly pipes could be hidden inside a handy little cabinet with the bowl set into it. It would not be long before the white fixtures would be replaced with coloured suites, dark blue, light blue, deep maroon, bright yellow and the later much reviled avocado. With these changes came new designs for lavatories – or toilets as the salesmen now called them. The greatest change came with incorporating the cistern into one with the lavatory bowl. Gone was the overhead cistern, originally cast iron with a chain, pulled to achieve the flushing system. These chains often ended with decorated porcelain knobs of different shapes and

designs. The porcelain lavatory bowls themselves were also bigger than the modern ones and often highly decorated inside. The seats varied from polished mahogany to serviceable scrubbed pine and their shapes from the curved overlapping 'throne' to the tightly-fitting lidded type. Away with such dated items, bring on the new, preferably in plastic, was the cry of the Sixties! The one thing missing from the 1960s bathroom was a shower. To most people showers had only been encountered in the local swimming baths, where before one entered the pool area one had to wade through a foot bath and also be sprinkled from a shower above. Similarly, one rinsed off the effects of the chlorinated pool water in a stronger shower at the end of the bathing session. Those pupils who had attended a school built in the 1930s which boasted a large sports field and a purpose-built gymnasium, and even in some cases its own swimming pool, will also have known the pleasure, or otherwise, of having to have a shower after a P.E. session. In many ways it is surprising that showers with their emphasis on economy both of water and its heating as well as requiring less space than a bath were not introduced much earlier into houses for the mass market. Perhaps, like meat and two veg, the bathtub was a necessity of life to the average Briton. However, the idea of using sprays did creep in slowly. The short rubber hosepipes with their twin sections that could be attached to the taps on the washbasin or the bath provided the means of achieving almost a salon-type shampoo for the modern young woman who often washed her hair more than the usual once a week. From there the move was towards providing a proper shower attachment to the bath taps but the idea of a separate shower cubicle was still a long way off.

While revelling in all the 'mod cons' their new houses brought them, 1960s women, particularly mothers of young children, were soon to discover that having the only lavatory in the house upstairs was somewhat of a drawback. Many of these women had lived in homes where, if indeed the bathroom itself had not been an extension off the kitchen, there was still an outside lavatory, which was very handy to use when children were outside playing in the garden or in the street. Now mothers were faced with a dilemma: did they insist that boots and shoes were taken off before the child ran upstairs, which could lead to 'accidents', or put up with dirt being brought in onto the carpets? Presumably it was to solve this problem that the cloakroom eventually became part of later designs, though some builders chose to place this amenity close to the front door rather than back one where it was most needed. Many homeowners took matters into their own hands and utilised the space in the cupboard under the stairs, knocking a door through from the kitchen to achieve the necessary 'downstairs' toilet.

Upstairs the layout of the average three-bedroom semi-detached house had changed little. There was the front room which was bigger than the other two and nowadays would be called the master bedroom. The second, which would just about take a double bed and not much else, was at the back while the third was often placed at the front of the house in the space above the hall, ideal for a cot and later a small bed. In some cases this little room lost space because it had to accommodate the rise in the stairs below. This would be disguised as a large box with a flat surface on top. Some builders placed a built-in cupboard above it, others left it for the occupants to do with what they would. Space was a problem. How much furniture did one need and how much could one realistically get in the space one had? One change that had come about was the sizing in beds. The double was the standard 4ft 6in but many couples made do with a 4ft bed which gave them a bit more space. For the smaller rooms twin beds were available in 3ft 6in, 3ft and 2ft 6in sizes, the last being ideal for a young child. Space was gained too, by replacing the metal coiled or mesh spring bed frames with their attached heavy woodenhead and footboards with a lightweight divan base that might or not have a headboard. For those who could not afford or did not wish to buy solid wood bedroom furniture, there was the option to buy the unpainted whitewood bedroom pieces from firms such as Liden. Certainly many young mothers furnished the nursery and later the child's bedroom with single wardrobes and chests of drawers with these. Liden was immensely popular during the Sixties and Seventies with its wide range of furniture advertised with the slogan 'You can paint it any colour you like', and people certainly did. There are homes today that still have pieces of Liden in use somewhere. The really enthusiastic handywoman and her man could equip their bedroom with self-assembly units consisting of wardrobes with sliding doors, a dressing table unit or a tallboy that would cover a whole wall.

Terence Conran is credited with introducing the continental quilt into his Habitat store in the mid-1960s. Travellers to Europe, particularly to Switzerland, Austria, Germany and the Nordic countries, were likely to have found one of these down-filled quilts on their chalet or hotel bed. Treated by many with great suspicion when they were imported into Britain, it was probably just as well, as they were very expensive. Most couples liked their crisp white sheets and pillowcases, the good British-made woollen blankets topped with a quilted eiderdown and matching counterpane. Many of these items were given as wedding presents – and had years of wear in them! The counterpane was the first to go, replaced during the 1960s by the heavy candlewick bedspread, either as a throw-over or neatly fitted, the latter perhaps being the most desirable to the house-proud wife, while the former could be more to the taste of the working woman who had not a great deal of time to make the bed neatly before leaving in the morning. Before the majority of us finally succumbed to the duvet, we had to go through the era of non-iron cotton sheets and worse still perhaps, the bri-nylon ones – warm in winter certainly but clingy and after constant washing they became covered in little bobbles all over them which rubbed against the skin as you slept.

Chapter Five

In the Kitchen

The 1960s took the kitchen of the past towards the more modern, streamlined affair that most of us recognise. A solid Victorian house would have had a breakfast room containing the coal-fired range on which most of the food was cooked. This room often served as a general living room for the family, the dining room and front parlour being reserved for Sundays and special occasions. Leading off the breakfast room was a much smaller room which housed on one wall the copper for washing days and the sink, which may or not have had a single cold tap over it, but would almost certainly have had a slatted wooden rack above where clean plates were left to dry. On the other wall would be a scrubbed wooden table for the preparation of food, above which ran a shelf that housed several saucepans, made of either copper or enamel. These either sat on the shelf or were suspended from it by hooks. As for the general storage of provisions that was catered for by yet a further small walk-in area, the larder. This had a stone floor and a small window that was covered by a mesh screen so that when it was open, flies and other insects were unable to enter. Where possible the larder would face north or east and since it was a single storey at the end of the house, it was reckoned to be the coldest part of the house.

With the coming of gas and electricity, the range became defunct and the new gas or electric cooker was moved into what had been the scullery, while the design of most houses built in the first half of the twentieth century had changed to front room, living/dining room and small galley kitchen which held little beyond the sink, cooker, a small table and possibly a cupboard which replaced the stone-floored larder. That there was so little storage space for either cooking utensils or food supplies may seem strange to people of the twenty-first century but the truth is the housewife of earlier times had made do with a limited amount of utensils, two or three saucepans, a mixing bowl and a pudding bowl, a cake and bun tins and a roasting tin that could be used for any number of dishes. Similarly, she did not keep large stocks of tinned foods in her cupboards; there were the basics such as treacle or golden syrup for the puddings she made, gravy browning or Oxo cubes, sugar, a pot of jam and another of marmalade, possibly peanut butter and of course a tin of baked beans. These, and flour and rice, were all replaced when necessary and other items such as tins of corned beef, tins of fruit, most likely to be pineapple chunks or peach slices, evaporated milk or tinned cream and the tin of best red salmon for very special occasions, were purchased when required. Most housewives shopped on a daily basis for fresh and perishable food and weekly for the main essentials. Most married women received housekeeping money on Friday evening after their husbands had received their pay packets and they quickly learnt how to budget to make it last so they could still put food on the table at the end of the week.

The Second World War and the immediate post-war years had brought rationing and shortages that meant adapting cooking and the preparation of meals to whatever was available. By the end of the 1950s, things had changed somewhat; imported goods were bringing foodstuffs that were either totally new to the general public or had been absent for many years. More and more foodstuffs were finding their way into tins so by the time we get to the Sixties, eating habits were beginning to change too and with them came the introduction of ready meals and fast food. Ironically as the 1960s kitchen evolved, becoming more streamlined with the emphasis on work surfaces overlying built-in cupboards and gadgets such as electric mixers, fridges and freezers, so the trend in home baking started to wane.

However, none of this happened overnight. For many families, meals in the Sixties were very much as they had been in the previous decade. S.E., who was thirteen in 1960, remembers clearly the pattern of meals in her home.

Dad left for work early so he and Mum had breakfast together, a boiled egg and bread and butter perhaps and cups of tea. I always left things till the last minute so I usually had marmalade sandwiches sitting at the table on my own while Mum 'hovered' because she was anxious I'd be late. We often had Kellogg's cornflakes on Saturday but on Sunday we all sat down together for a fried breakfast of egg, bacon and bread. We had a cooked meal midday and tea in the evening when Dad got home – he had a cooked meal in the canteen at work.

The routine went like this. Monday (washday) was cold sliced roast beef with potatoes and baked beans and a cold fruit tart or pie with custard. Tea would be sandwiches and cakes and cups of tea. Tuesday (housework & finishing drying the washing) dinner was usually minced meat patty with baked potatoes, tinned fruit and evaporated milk (for afters!). Wednesday (ironing & airing of linen – very important in those days) dinner, pork chops cooked in the oven with gravy and onions with mashed potatoes and cabbage or cauliflower. Mum used to make a baked suet pudding and this was usually served first with the gravy, then the meat and vegetables. We might have been lucky and had a Penguin biscuit afterwards. Alternatively on Wednesday we might have a beef casserole with dumplings, or a meat pudding. Thursday we had sausages and mash and baked beans with a steamed sponge pudding with custard. Friday morning Mum would take her order book to the Co-op for the groceries to be delivered and also to the butcher, who delivered on Saturday mornings. On her way home she would call at the fishmongers' to buy fish and we would have home-cooked fish and chips for dinner followed by rice pudding. I didn't like rice pudding so I had sliced or mashed banana and custard. Friday afternoon Mum did all her baking of cakes for the week. Dad worked until twelve on Saturday, so that was the day we had roast beef and Yorkshire pudding, the pudding coming first with gravy then the meat and vegetables. After that Dad would go to the Football Match when they were playing at home while Mum, my sister and I would go shopping in town and meet up with Dad after the match and we'd all walk home together. Later Dad would go down the road to the paper shop and wait for the 'Green'un', the football paper with all the results in it and he would bring back home a block of ice cream. After tea, which in winter would be bread toasted in front of the coal fire and spread with butter and jam, we would all sit round and eat the ice cream, sliced and sandwiched between two wafers and listen to the radio. On Sunday, after church, dinner would be cold beef and vegetables followed by one of Mum's apple tarts with either custard or cream. Tea would be salad with tinned salmon or celery and cheese, a trifle, if we had visitors, and homemade cakes, of course.

That menu, or variations of it, was to be found the length and breadth of the country. Sunday tea in particular was the time when one entertained, usually relations or very close friends. That was the time when the finest tablecloth was laid and the best tea service was brought out of the china cabinet and often there were insufficient chairs to go round so the piano stool and the old kitchen chair might be pressed into service. Many a young man in the early 1960s who received an invitation to his girlfriend's home for Sunday Tea knew that this might be make-or-break time in the relationship as he received the full scrutiny of her parents.

As the decade progressed, slowly the old patterns began to change. Shops and offices no longer closed for an hour or two in the middle of the day, and neither did factories stop production at dinnertime as they had in the past. Soon it was well-nigh impossible for workers, in whatever field, to return home for a cooked midday meal. Schools found that by providing meals on the premises, they too could manage to squeeze in an extra lesson in the morning. So began the trend for workers to eat sandwiches brought from home in a shortened break and for the evening meal to become much more substantial than it had been. The stay-at-home wife had to readjust her working day; instead of spending the morning cooking a hot dinner, this was now put off till the afternoon. Many found that meals that required long, slow cooking like casseroles and steamed puddings could be made first thing and then left to take care of themselves. The women who worked often used the lunch hour to shop for the ingredients for the meal they would cook when they got home. Without people realising it, the evening meal still known as 'tea' in some homes, or 'supper' or 'dinner' in others, was gradually being eaten later in the day.

For a time housewives still bought fresh food on an almost daily basis and cooked meals from scratch but as more and more convenience foods became available, so people were tempted to try them. Why, ran the argument, should you go to all the trouble of going to the butcher and buying meat to cook and spend precious time making pastry when you could buy a pie in a tin? All that was needed was for you to use your tin opener to remove the lid, pop it into the oven, and there was the basis of a family meal needing only a few potatoes and some vegetables to finish it off. Not only a saving in time and effort but no dirty pie dish to wash up at the end of the meal – the tin went straight in the dustbin. The array of meat products available in tins was formidable. Many of the 1960s housewives had been brought up eating Spam and corned beef but now there was a wide choice; ham came in large and small tins, accompanied by deliciously-flavoured jelly; tongues too; from Australia came tinned mutton loaf which made a very good filling for a plate pie as well as being good mashed up with tomato sauce in sandwiches or sliced with salad. Tins of chunks of beef, lamb and chicken, some with and others without diced vegetables but all with gravy, gave the housewife plenty of choice. A particular favourite was the large tin which contained a whole cooked chicken. At around £1 a tin, this was expensive but as a treat or for a special occasion like Christmas, it was extremely good value. It could also provide the basis for a number of meals on a family camping holiday as it could be eaten cold or heated up in a tin of chicken soup in a saucepan over a primus stove or camp fire. Similarly, the range of fish products available in tins was growing. Sardines and pilchards, the one in oil, the other in tomato sauce, served on toast in wintertime had always been a standby for high tea and of course, there was that great standby, a tin of red salmon. That had always been relatively expensive but now there was a paler competitor, pink salmon and by the mid-Sixties a newcomer on the scene, the now ubiquitous tinned tuna. For those on a very tight budget, this was an inexpensive alternative to salmon and provided the ingenious housewife with opportunities to create different dishes. Whatever else the 1960s bride collected in her bottom drawer ready for setting up house, she needed to make sure that she had a good tin opener!

However, there was competition now in the form of packets of dried meals that only required water to turn them into tempting meals. A surprising number of the younger contributors mentioned Vesta curries in the Sixties. For the woman who normally cooked her left-over meat as mince these packets would have been anathema since she had long been able to turn out a reasonable curry simply by the addition of a teaspoonful or so of curry powder, Vencatachellums' for preference, an apple and a handful of sultanas. As for the rice she served with it, that may have been the same sort she used for rice pudding; long grain, Basmati, Patna and others types may have been on sale in specialist grocery stores in large cities but they were not generally available.

Foreign holidays to Italy in the late Fifties and Sixties, however, had introduced British travellers to a whole different way not only of cooking but of eating too. To most women of the period the word 'pasta' was relatively unknown, although they were acquainted with spaghetti and macaroni. For many, inch-long pieces of spaghetti came in a meat sauce in a tin – and had a tinny taste. It was usually eaten on toast as a teatime meal. Macaroni had always been around, it seemed, featuring regularly on school-dinner menus throughout the 1940s and 1950s as a milk pudding. Macaroni cheese was also a popular dish when meat was in short supply. But now holidaymakers discovered that spaghetti could be as much as a foot long and was frequently eaten at the beginning of a meal rather than as the main dish. Not only that, the term pasta now covered a wide and exciting variety that included ravioli, sheets for lasagne, and all the other shapes and thickness. They discovered too that the Italians used tomatoes in cooking to great effect where we Britons tended to think of them purely as a salad ingredient or perhaps served occasionally fried with bacon and eggs and a slice of fried bread.

Perhaps the greatest discovery was the use of olive oil. This was almost totally unknown in the average British kitchen. If it was found anywhere in the house it would have been in a small bottle obtained from the chemist and kept in the medicine cabinet. A few drops warmed could be poured into the ear to alleviate severe earache. Alternatively, food connoisseurs would use a few drops when making vinaigrette dressing for their salad – not like the majority who poured small amounts of Heinz salad cream over their lettuce, cucumber and tomato. Olive oil had to be imported and was very much a luxury item, so it would be some time before it was being regularly used.

One of the best ways of discovering trends in the 1960s kitchen is to look through women's magazines of the period. A monthly magazine for September 1964 devotes its cookery section to what could almost be a spin-off for part of television's *Great British Bake-Off* in the form of ten variations of a basic sponge cake ranging from the two layers through to a Swiss Roll, Gateaux, Torte and everything in between. For those daunted by such magnificent concoctions there was also instruction on how to make smaller versions such as lemon and ginger spice bars cooked in a Swiss Roll tin and the ubiquitous cupcake which was cooked in a deep bun tin. Current devotees of this particular sponge cake may be interested to learn that the directions for making them states that they should be turned upside down to cool and when cold should have a swirl of icing topped with a sliced peach on what we now regard as the bottom of the cake. The only other cookery item in this issue was a recipe to help use up the glut of apples the cook might have in her garden. The apple slice used a slab of frozen puff pastry covered with sliced apples, cooked on a Swiss Roll tin.

Most of the magazines aimed at women had their own regular cookery writers; these sensible, down-to-earth women quickly established a rapport with their readers. Fifty years on, their voices on the faded page not only inspire confidence but also give modern readers a glimpse of past eating habits and some clues as to when items first came into use. An illustrated selection of recipes suggested how to turn valuable scraps into tempting hot meals, thus revealing many items that rarely appear on the tables of modern homes and only very occasionally in specialist restaurants. Osso Buco, a dish based on a shin of veal (and the popular Weiner schnitzel or veal escalope) is a reminder that veal, once very much a part of the British diet, disappeared from sale after the outcry against the methods of raising young dairy bull calves for slaughter. Although still much in evidence on the Continent, only a handful of farmers in this country produce veal in any quantity, thus the meat is not to be found in supermarkets or in many butchers' shops. It may find its way on to the menu of high-class restaurants but it is no longer the very popular and reasonably-priced meat it was for several generations. The recipe for Osso Buco includes tomato puree in the ingredients. This was certainly available in small tins in London shops in the 1950s but not necessarily to be found all over the country. Sensibly, the recipe writer advises that tomato ketchup would do as well – and what home in the 1960s was without its bottle of Heinz Tomato Ketchup? Mention was made earlier about the different types of rice and in this recipe we are informed it should be Patna.

How many of today's cooks would either recognise or know how to deal with sweetbreads? So squeamish have we become that many cannot even bear to consider from what part of the animal these have come. Light and delicate in flavour – once much recommended as being suitable for invalids – we are given ideas for using them in two dishes; either as a fricassee, which includes the addition of a packet of frozen peas; or the more substantial fried sweetbreads with streaky bacon, served with toast. The mention of frozen peas reminds us they were the first vegetable to be treated in this way and for domestic use were available in small quantities as the use of the term 'packet' suggests. Even by 1969 not everyone had a refrigerator large enough to store frozen foods. The small domestic fridge, which fitted under a worktop or often stood beside the cooker and had a handy worktop of its own that provided extra space for dishes to stand on, had only the small compartment at the top of the interior which housed the ice-making unit but left a space large enough to take a block of ice cream or packets of peas but little else. Small domestic freezers were still in their infancy and were very expensive. Those who wanted to make use of a freezer, either because they had a large garden or allotment and had gluts of fruit and vegetables, or wished to be able to do large batch baking of dishes they could freeze to eat later, found the way to solve the problem of cost was to buy a large commercial chest freezer which did not carry the same high purchase tax. Since few kitchens were big enough to take these large machines, they were often housed in the garage or outhouse.

The fact that supermarkets do stock liver in the butchery section shows that that at least is still with us, although possibly not used, as the cookery writer would suggest, as a casserole with butter beans, carrots and swedes. Ox kidney, however, is a different story. There was a time in the Fifties and Sixties when our mothers and grandmothers made meat puddings with suet crusts. When they bought the stewing beef, skirt or shin, the butcher would, if asked, include a chunk of ox kidney for a few extra pence while the lump of suet required for the pudding would often come gratis. These days, it is well-nigh impossible to buy ox kidney; the butcher may suggest one uses pig's kidney instead but that definitely does not taste the same. Incidentally it has been noted that some supermarkets now label it 'pork' liver rather than pig's. Squeamishness or political correctness? The recipe using ox kidney was for an open pie using a puff-pastry base. It was a surprise to find that it was by then taken for granted that the pastry was both bought and frozen. Instructive too, is that having given directions on how to cook the pastry base, we are then told that we can make this in advance and store it in a polythene bag for several days. When required, all you needed to do was place it in an oven – gas mark 6, electric 400°F for ten minutes – and then add the kidney filling. If ox kidney was considered too strong a flavour, then one could make a very novel dish of kebabs using lambs' kidneys wrapped in streaky bacon interspersed with small pieces of bananas similarly enclosed in bacon. The kebabs were then cooked under the grill. By 1969 eye-level grills had grown both in popularity and use and some enterprising companies had introduced spits into them – though one suspects that was a novelty that soon wore off.

Pressure cookers had been in use in many homes since the Fifties and many cooks swore that whatever was cooked by this method tasted much fresher, and was more tender. This was the suggested method for a casserole using ox-tail, though slow cooking in the oven would serve just as well. Reading the recipe nowadays one is struck by the use of dripping as the recommended fat for sealing the pieces of meat. The fact that the magazine was issued in 1969 shows that many housewives were still doing as their mothers had and saving the fat juices which came from the roast beef joint. Quite apart from its use as a fat, dripping will revive memories for those who had it spread on their toast in winter. Delicious too was the jelly that formed under the layer of fat. In those far-off days lard was the chosen form of cooking fat, whether it be in pastry or for frying or roasting. Each time a joint was cooked, the lard which had basted it, mixed with its natural fat and juices left in the pan was poured into the dripping bowl. It was added to and used again and again, being kept, before refrigerators, in the larder with a muslin cloth over the top to keep flies off. It was not just the introduction of other cooking fats which led to the demise of the dripping bowl but new ideas on food hygiene decried the reuse of cooking fats, even those kept in the refrigerator, despite the fact that one rarely heard of anyone getting food poisoning from dripping. But back to our ox-tail casserole! Once it had been cooked and most of it eaten, the remains could be turned into soup – waste not want not – using a liquidiser if one was fortunate enough to have such a gadget or a mouli. These hand-held sieves with a handle which squashed the contents through the sieve were extremely popular in the Sixties both for culinary purposes and also for making purees of vegetables and other foods for babies when the weaning process began.

Other offal dishes such as tripe and onions were included – the only interesting point in that recipe being the use of '1 large packet of instant mash potato'. Those who were watching commercial television in the 1970s will recall the advertising campaign featuring the 'Martians' who extolled the virtues of Smash. Cadbury's, better known in those days for confectionery, had introduced Smash in the mid-1960s. The earliest version, Pom, came from Coleman's of mustard fame who in 1946 produced a commercial film shown in cinemas starring the well-known actor of the period Jack Hulbert and his wife demonstrating how to reconstitute the dried potato flour into mash. The product was introduced with him singing a tune with the words 'Pom, pom, tiddly pom' and so it became known. At that time in the immediate post-war period and for the decade that followed it was probably used most in canteens, for the idea of using dehydrated potato granules took time to catch on with the average housewife, yet here it was, being recommended by a respected cookery writer. The three remaining dishes in the feature on offal were for an ox heart stew, strangely not the stuffed recipe which had once been so popular; instead the writer advised stuffing lambs' hearts which were much smaller and her final offering was deep-fried sheep's brains in butter!

The magazine included two other items on cookery. First was a cake with directions on how to achieve the most elaborate icing decoration, which would turn it into a 'basket of flowers cake'. A more practical menu for the impending Easter Weekend was also included. Sunday lunch was roast chicken served with potatoes and braised button onions with a fruit pie or milk pudding for dessert. What made the potatoes special was that after peeling they were left whole and parboiled, then each was sliced almost through, before being packed, cuts upwards, closely together in an ovenproof dish, the bottom of which was covered with stock. Butter was dotted over the potato tops; seasoning and a bay leaf were added before a close-fitting lid was put on and the dish placed in the oven on the shelf below the chicken. Note, no mention was made of any other vegetable to be served with this. It should however, be pointed out that to many people a fresh chicken was still regarded as a luxury for special occasions. Easter Monday's offering was basically a macaroni cheese to which was added the leftover bits of chicken

Leaving tradition behind, this was the very latest style for wedding dresses c. 1962.

WEST LODGE PARK
HADLEY WOOD
NEAR BARNET · HERTS
TELEPHONE: 01-449 9293

17th February, 1969.

Wedding Reception
15th February 1969.

To 76 Lunches @ 27/6	104.	10.	0.
103 Sherries @ 3/6	18.	0.	6.
16 Entre deux Mers @ 21/-	16.	16.	0.
4 Santos Rose @ 27/6	5.	10.	0.
10 Raphael @ 44/6	22.	5.	0.
1 Jug Fruit Cup @ 10/6		10.	6.
	167.	12.	0.
10% Staff Gratuities	16.	15.	0.
	184.	7.	0.
To Room Hire	3.	3.	0.
Flowers	5.	5.	0.
Changing Room	2.	2.	0.
40 Players		12.	2.
40 Perfectos		12.	2.
	£196.	1.	4.
Less Deposit	10.	0.	0.
	£185.	6.	4.

This very detailed invoice for a wedding reception in 1969 shows how prices increased during the decade.

The invoice for the fashionable teak bedroom suite does not include the bed itself.

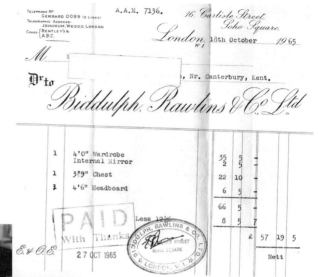

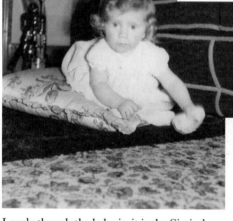

Lovely though the baby is, it is the Sixties' furnishings that are of interest. Note the patterned carpet, tiled fireplace and the very popular 'Gladiator' companion set as the fire-irons were called.

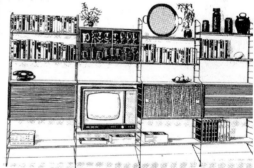

With this versatile ladder system, one could customise shelves and units to suit one's own needs and taste. They were very fashionable in the new open-plan living rooms.

The memorable freezing winter of 1963. This was the scene on 31 December 1962. Much more snow was to follow.

During the winter of 1963 a group of Suffolk students went on an Outward Bound course to Wales.

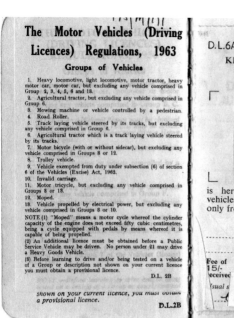

That precious driving licence that gave women their freedom.

The Morris Minor 1000 was probably the most popular car in the 1960s. Here we have R., who was encouraged to learn to drive as soon as she was old enough, in the school uniform she wore to take her test.

AUSTIN DISTRIBUTORS
INVOICE
45 SOUTH ST. Tilleys (DORSET) LTD. DORCHESTER

Telephone : Dorchester 414 (4 lines).   Telegrams : "Motors Dorchester."

M .... Mrs Hutchinson
9 Weatherby Way
Dorchester

SERVED BY .... STK553   DATE 16.6.67
ORDER No. .... STK553   PER ....

5 gals Super Shell   petrol   £1 5 5

E. & O. E.   £ 1 5 5
10% handling charge made for goods returned after 7 days
THIS INVOICE No. MUST BE QUOTED WHEN PARTS ARE RETURNED FOR CREDIT
59637   BESLEYS INTERFAN, EXETER

Those were the days, when petrol was around five shillings (25p) a gallon (approx. 4·5 litres). Five gallons almost filled the Austen Mini's tank.

A very determined-looking J.T. on her large scooter. Young women loved the freedom they gave.

An example of the small advertisements which appeared in women's magazines. These show that many women were still making not only their own clothes but household items too. The corsetry item catered for those large-waisted women who were unable to buy garments their size in the shops.

This shows the summer fashions that were available both in shops and by post (a forerunner of on-line shopping) in the Sixties.

Sixth-form girls out of uniform, ready for an evening at the theatre at Stratford-upon-Avon. It is likely they were all wearing the fashionable stiffened petticoats to make their skirts stand out.

Such was the interest in music in the Sixties that even the very young were playing records on the popular portable players. In this rather minimalist living room we see that television sets have grown in size since the 1950s.

In the summer term of 1961, a group of A-level students set off from Dorset in a bus with its lady driver to spend five days on a tour of Shakespeare country, including a visit to the newly-restored Coventry Cathedral and a Jane Austen day in Bath.

G. in her pushchair being wheeled ashore after the long voyage with other migrants to Australia in 1960.

How small this aircraft about to start on a long-haul flight from Nigeria to Heathrow seems compared to the aircraft of today.

I say "A Guinness a day keeps the doctor away"

f I had my way it'd be on the National Health—Guinness I mean. You should ee me on a Friday, when I've just done he weekend shopping—it's down with the shopping bags, feet up and a glass of Guinness. By the time the kids get in from school I'm fighting fit again — and believe me, I need to be!

That's Jack and me dancing at the Five Bells. We always have a night out on our wedding anniversary.

That was taken when we were away last year. It was the first holiday for years when we actually got away on our own. But the weather...brrr!

GUINNESS
is good for ~~you~~ me

An unusual Guinness advertisement in that it was aimed specifically at women and the benefits it could bring to their health. During the 1960s nursing mothers were often encouraged to drink stout but the advert suggests that all women could benefit from a Guinness.

from the day before and a tin of asparagus spears. The last was also regarded as a luxury item. Obviously, everyone must have been suffering from a surfeit of Easter Eggs, or was it Hot Cross Buns, because after the pasta, it was suggested that fresh fruit should be served.

In the very early Sixties entertaining at home was mostly for family and very close friends and usually on Sundays for tea or for special occasions. Although wartime Britain had seen people open their homes to entertain Servicemen, this habit did not become ingrained nor was it extended to strangers, with the exception perhaps of church members. People liked to keep themselves to themselves. Nowhere is this better typified than in S.E.'s description of what happened in 1969 after she and her new husband left at 5 p.m. to catch the train to Ilfracombe for their honeymoon. Around sixty guests, mainly members of the extended families on both sides had waved them off having just enjoyed a three-course meal at a local hotel. Then 'my family members went back to my parents' house for the evening and my husband's family went back to his parents' home. No discos then!' What is interesting is that this happened up and down the country where the bride and groom lived in the same town. It was not just that the two families were stand-offish and did not wish to fraternise with the other side – though there may have been some of that – but homes were rarely big enough to take all the guests who wished to stay on, but also, a wedding, like a funeral, was very much an excuse for families who might rarely meet to get together. S.E. also commented that the only outsiders included on the wedding guest list were her two close friends.

It was in the Sixties that more and more young men and women were living far away from their parental home. Those who had studied had made friends with fellow students while those who were working made new acquaintances through the workplace, perhaps with those who occupied a bedsitter in a multi-occupancy house or through a sports activity. Meeting in a coffee bar or the local pub gave an opportunity for general conversation but what better way to get to know someone than to invite them back to 'my place' for a cup of coffee or a beer after work. From this small beginning came the 'drinks' party. Students had already developed a taste for the 'bring a bottle' type of gathering, usually Merrydown cider or beer. Knowing that no one was 'rolling in money', most parties were of this type and only rarely included a very small bottle of spirits but more likely a cheap British sherry or, daringly, a bottle of Dubonnet. At this sort of party the only edible offerings would be crisps – until 1962 only salted or salt and vinegar; cheese and onion and then smoky bacon flavours appeared in the shops during the latter half of the Sixties. As these young folk became more sophisticated the drinks party became more formal; rather than the spontaneous or casual affair, one now issued actual invitations for early-evening drinks for an hour or so before each guest was expected to go home to eat. If the invitation came from people one did not know very well, particularly a higher-ranking work colleague, then one dressed for the affair, a pretty cocktail dress – the balloon skirt was fashionable or that little black dress. A choice of red or white wine would be on offer, and to stave or the pangs of hunger (because this was past your usual meal time) there would also be snacks. These included the now much derided small cubes of cheddar cheese skewered on a cocktail stick and stuck into an inverted half grapefruit which might, if the hostess was really inventive, have been covered in silver foil. When completed, the half grapefruit was supposed to look like a hedgehog. An added refinement was to add a cube of pineapple to the end of the cocktail stick and, if the hosts were really trendy, the pineapple might be replaced with a maraschino cherry or even – an olive. Also on offer would be sausage rolls – warmed at the beginning of the evening – cheese straws, Scotch eggs and cocktail sausages on sticks. Some of these items would have been made by the hostess, so the quality rather depended on her skill, especially with pastry which, no doubt would have been of the frozen puff variety.

Amongst the young couples living in new areas and making new friends, a more casual form of entertaining developed. Sometimes, on the spur of the moment, a husband, after playing football, rugby or hockey on a Saturday afternoon, would bring home a lonely bachelor friend to share the couple's supper. One contributor recalls stretching the spaghetti bolognese and following it with banana custard. While 'spag bol' was her signature dish, another friend only served gammon and pineapple with chocolate mousse or lemon meringue pie. It was the young professional women who led the way, experimenting with new dishes which they wished to show off, to the new wave of supper or dinner parties which became a feature of life in the second half of the 1960s. By this time many of them had television sets in their homes so they were able to learn how to create suitable dishes by watching Fanny Craddock's weekly cookery programmes. Just as in recent times when one praised a meal in a friend's house, she might reply 'it's one of Delia's' so in the Sixties one would hear 'it's one of Fanny Craddock's'. To this day there are women around who remember her dismissive remark when garnishing a seafood cocktail, that one must make sure that one did not end up with a prawn hanging over the side looking seasick. Her cutting remarks and her bullying of her husband Johnny and the young trainees who did the dirty work in the studio, made her a force to be reckoned with – but she taught a whole generation not only how to cook but also how to entertain.

Invited out to supper or dinner – the latter tended to be a bit more formal with the best wedding present silver and china, not to mention the damask table napkins which normally stayed in the sideboard drawer – you were likely to eat a fairly predictable meal. For starters any one of the following might be served. The aforementioned prawn cocktail was not only very popular it was also fairly safe, both for the cook to prepare and the diner to eat. Potted shrimps with thin toast or a salmon mousse; a slice of melon prepared so that the slices slipped out on alternate sides and either sprinkled with sugar (out came the silver sugar sifter!) and powdered ginger or the ginger was served separately. Only the real connoisseurs produced crystallised ginger in syrup. An alternative fruit was the half grapefruit topped with a glacé cherry. If soup was served it was most likely to be French onion. At the more formal dinner a fish course of scampi, salmon, sole or smoked haddock might be served. But it was with the meat course that the hostess (and Fanny Craddock) really went to town. Would it be peppered steak and chips – a dish surely undertaken for only a few or Coq au Vin? Duck and orange sauce, Beef Goulash, a Crown of Lamb, Sweet and Sour Pork Chops or Weiner Schnitzel? Puddings varied from fresh fruit salad; cheesecake, often the baked variety – none of the bashed biscuit base with a packet mix filling; pineapple upside down cake; a soufflé – very risky that; Black Forest gateau; lemon meringue pie, made from scratch or mandarin orange cream pie. What a blessing those tinned mandarin oranges were! The very mention of this pie brings back memories of boiling up evaporated milk still in its tin – with a hole in the top – and when it was really thick mixing it into an orange jelly which was close to setting.

These were all dishes that one would pay good money for in a first-class restaurant, yet here were ordinary women producing fine-quality food. The 1960s produced many items for the kitchen or dining table which once would have been found in the homes of the rich. The ordinary housewife who had long made do with enamel or aluminium saucepans was now looking to buy the heavy cast-iron dishes and pans in bright colours which featured on TV, or she who had always been happy to use the old-fashioned tin opener with the corkscrew in the handle now wanted the one that fitted on the side of the tin, was wound round and removed the lid without leaving a jagged edge. Better still was the one that fitted on the wall and electrically removed the lid, a godsend if one used a lot of tins when preparing a meal! There was, without a doubt, a great deal of one-upmanship or keeping up with the Joneses when it came to kitchen equipment – 'You mix it up in the Kenwood, dear. Oh, you don't have the complete version, do you?' Then there was how was the best way to serve coffee at the end of a meal. You were already at an advantage if you were able to grind your own beans and thus make your own blend. Then it was a case of do you use an electric percolator – so useful because you could have it plugged in on the sideboard – or did you use your attractive pottery coffee set, pouring boiling water straight on to the beans at the bottom of the pot with its matching jug for those who liked warm milk with their coffee. Possibly you were one of those who preferred to stand your Cona coffee maker on the sideboard so that guests could watch the water passing over the ground coffee and into the jug below. It is possible that many women of the 1960s, when faced nowadays with the task of downsizing from their family home, have discovered, stowed at the back of some infrequently-used cupboard, many relics that had once seemed essential for entertaining, which brings us to the fondue set, originally designed on the Continent as a way of melting a selection of cheeses with wine in a small saucepan which stood on a trivet in the middle of the table. Below the pan was a tiny spirit stove which produced enough heat to melt the contents of the fondue pot. Everyone seated at the table was given a long fork, a bit like a very thin toasting fork, and the idea was that one would impale a piece of bread on the end and then dip it into the cheese mixture. The 1960s variation on this was the Fondue Bourguignonne. Steak replaced the cheese and each guest, preferably not more than six of you all together, was given a dish containing half a pound of rump steak, which you will have asked the butcher to cut into bite-size cubes. Around the tray on which the fondue set stood the hostess would have arranged a number of dishes: tinned anchovies, olives, gherkins, pineapple chunks and bananas and a mayonnaise base for tomato, curry, mustard and herb sauces. Chunks of fresh bread should also be available. The fondue forks that accompanied the sets usually had different coloured markings on them so each guest knew which was theirs when they plunged their piece of steak into the hot fat or oil for cooking. If one had the misfortune to lose the piece of meat in the pot, some people enlivened the proceedings by demanding that the loser perform a forfeit. This form of entertaining could be great fun, but experience taught that it was best to choose one's guests carefully. Older gentlemen in particular saw it as a terrible waste of a good steak.

Of course not everyone lived the 'high life' of fancy food and dinner parties. Quite apart from those who could not afford such things but still managed to feed their families with the best they could, there were still families throughout the country living in remote rural areas who had little access to many culinary items that they would have been unable to prepare had they been able to get them. It is difficult in the twenty-first century to believe that less than fifty years ago there were places where there was neither electricity, gas nor water and sewage available to their homes. Eventually electricity would come to most of them but the likelihood of a gas pipe reaching them is still, for many, a long way in the future. To those living in such areas, they depended for years on paraffin oil to give them light and to heat the ovens that resembled the gas stove they would never have. For a long time country women continued to cook on the coal-fired range as their grandmothers had done but this meant having a fire going the whole time. Those who could afford it had an Aga, again coal-fired until the advent of oil-fired models. Instead of looking back and perhaps commiserating with the poor countrywomen who had to produce food in such 'antiquated' kitchens, we should congratulate them for producing some of the best cookery in the country.

Most of the women who wrote about food agreed that learning how to cook was something that on the whole did not come naturally.

[We married in 1968] My husband was used to being served a full roast with two sorts of potatoes and five (!) vegetables every lunchtime followed by apple pie and custard, which his mother had waiting for him. He only had half an hour for his break. So when we married, despite having cookery GCE, I felt I was unable to come up to the mark, so took myself off to Smith's to buy a cookery book. This was a result of burning the sausages I had fried him for lunch on the first day back from our honeymoon. I was not too concerned about my lack of skill though, and encouraged his mother when she suggested leaving a chocolate cake for her dear boy on a regular basis. I think she thought him deprived. To be frank, I was really not interested in cooking but soon learned in an effort to please my husband.

That sentiment probably applied to most married women. Thus it was that the standard of cooking generally improved during the Sixties and slowly the innovations percolated down to the older generation of cooks who began to experiment too, although some of them had a difficult task in persuading their husbands to try different foods or more familiar ones prepared in a different manner.

Chapter Six

Memorable Events of the 1960s

Women were asked a very generalised question as to which major national or world events had had an impact on them at the time. These were among the things that worried them.

The Cold War

This began in 1947 but by the beginning of the Sixties the struggle for supremacy between the United States and the USSR had intensified to dangerous proportions. The United Kingdom seemed to be caught in the middle, especially vulnerable as the US had reopened or expanded their airbases on British soil. The threat of a nuclear war which had been a feature of the second half of the 1950s, now seemed much more real. Several women mentioned their fears during the Cuban Missile Crisis of 1962 in particular. However, nearer home in Europe the Soviet-controlled East Berlin was closed off from the west by the erection of the infamous Berlin Wall in 1961.

> Political events had little effect on me except for the Berlin Wall that went up and closed when my husband and I were on holiday in West Berlin. We found ourselves trapped as we had gone into Berlin by train through one of the three corridors that went into East Germany. These corridors were promptly closed when the wall went up. Our only way out was by air which was difficult to organise and expensive as so many people were trying to leave Berlin.

The Campaign For Nuclear Disarmament

CND, as it was always known, had been formed in 1957 by a number of leading churchmen, politicians, writers and actors as well as ordinary people who were worried by the proliferation of nuclear establishments throughout the country and the storage of missiles at American airbases. Local branches held meetings, and membership, which was strongly middle class, grew throughout the Sixties. Protests were to be of a peaceful nature, taking the form of orderly marches. The highlight of the campaign was the annual four-day Easter March from the UK's Atomic Weapons Establishment at Aldermaston to London. Most women indicated that they had sympathies with CND but very few of them actually joined the marches.

I was a member of CND for several years and took part in local protests at Sellafield [nuclear power station] and Barrow and even went to a CND march in London. In the 1960s Sellafield posed a real threat to Cumbria (and the country, I suppose) because of its questionable safety standards, so it was a hot topic them (no pun intended). But it was also one of the two main employers for Millom so protest wasn't popular.

I did get quite involved with protesting. I can remember my father saying he'd make me a banner that just said 'I Protest' as I don't think I was too fussy about which marches I went on. I was probably spurred on a bit by Brian Bird (the local vicar) who was quite an activist. I remember marches in London; Aldermaston marches (although I never went all the way to Aldermaston) and anti-Vietnam marches, until they started getting scary.

I supported CND but rather from the sidelines – my Dad would not let me join in marches.

Any contact with CND would have been severely frowned on by my parents as they both served in the Royal Navy during World War Two.

We were members of CND and joined a protest outside the shipyard in Barrow-in-Furness. It was a candle-lit vigil lasting from about 8 p.m. to midnight. There were a lot of policemen mixing among the crowd, but as far as I remember there was no trouble.

I was aware of CND and briefly got entangled with the Animal Liberation Front and the hunt Saboteurs. Decided I wasn't cut out for activities that brushed with the law so didn't take part in any events.

I worried about the bomb. The Cuba crisis in the winter of 1962 was extremely frightening. I was living in a YWCA hostel in Mornington

Crescent at the time and I remember going to bed one night convinced that I would be obliterated by a nuclear bomb before the next morning came. The atmosphere in London was very tense and I was petrified. Fortunately it didn't happen but the nuclear threat was a worry all through the decade.

Fog and the Winter of 1963

I have vivid memories of the last London fog of December **1962** ... I remember the air inside the hostel getting more and more opaque as the days went on. It got to the stage that you could hardly see across the room. In the streets, men were walking in front of the red London buses carrying flaming torches made of oily rags on poles to guide the buses through the smog. It must have lasted at least a week and, at the end of it, I had to throw out my only petticoat, which had become so black from soot particles that it couldn't be washed clean! It was very dramatic but I think that a lot of people died from the foul air and it prompted the introduction of smokeless fuel for household fires.

Very few people were unaffected by the severe winter of **1963**. In many parts of the country snow started falling just before the old year came to an end. In the early 1960s we did not have the sophisticated weather forecasting available today and although those with television sets were able to see what might happen in their area the next day, most people who needed to know, like farmers, gardeners and travellers, listened to the brief weather reports on the radio. Perhaps it was because it was still a festive time that we were taken by surprise when we woke that Sunday morning to find the world had turned white.

It was 30 December and my birthday. Being Sunday, there weren't the usual traffic noises of cars taking people to work, so it came as a complete shock when I looked out and saw nothing but a blanket of snow. I had arranged to have a drinks party at lunchtime for friends and neighbours and panicked, wondering what on earth I would do with all those sausage rolls, vol au vents and other nibbles I'd made last night. Funnily enough, it turned out to be the best party I've ever given. Everyone came wrapped up and Wellington booted, one couple arrived on skis but the highlight was the arrival of my sister with my young nephew. They didn't live far away but she and her husband had solved the problem of transporting their one year old by lifting the pram body off its wheels and turning it into a sledge they could pull.

So it was fun! Yes, until the novelty wore off and more snow fell and then it froze solid bringing with it a multitude of problems that included towns and villages being cut off as minor roads were impassable; frozen points on the railways; power cuts; burst pipes; and food shortages, particularly vegetables – potatoes and root vegetables could not be lifted from the ground, greens like sprouts and cabbages froze in the fields. Other goods could not be moved from one area to another; coal and petrol supplies became desperately low in some parts of the country, it was, said those who remembered, just like the 1940s all over again.

I remember the winter of 1963; roads covered with deep snow which had frozen. All the coal stocks were frozen and roads and rail too, so coal merchants couldn't make deliveries. Our oven was electric so I had to ask our neighbour to cook our evening meal on her gas stove, as there were power cuts too. Then, we took our candles, food and portable radio to friends a couple of times as obviously their TV and mains radio were out of action.

In the dreadful freezing winter of 1963 our underground pipes froze and we were without running water for three weeks. Our kindly next-door neighbours allowed us to fill up a few buckets of water each day. Our meagre coal fire (lit only in the evenings) was quite inadequate in heating our very cold sitting room and the rest of the house. Cycled to work on icy roads, still wearing stiletto heels and slid off when a few months pregnant close to the Docks which were frozen over.

The long, hard winter of 1962/3 was the worst I have ever known. The big difficulty for us was getting coal and pink paraffin.

The winter of 1963 was really bad. I can remember it because it started on New Year's Eve and went on until the beginning of April. I had to walk to work about three miles every day and home again and got through about four pairs of boots, and when the snow and ice cleared we had really bad fog [this was in London] so everyone had bad coughs. I don't think I have ever seen the like again.

I managed to get a place in the GFS [Girls' Friendly Society] hostel in the centre of Birmingham. This was great – cheap, friendly and basic. We shared three to a bedroom. It was freezing cold in that winter of 1962/63; smog would fill the rooms even.

I remember that the train couldn't run from Weymouth to Dorchester on the night it snowed. I think the Ridgeway tunnel was blocked. Not sure how we got to Dorchester the next day but remember the walk from there to Charminster where I descended on my Granny for the night. Don't know how long it took me to get home where my Mum was on her own breaking the ice on the cattle trough and wading through snowdrifts to feed the poultry with hot water bottles strapped to her waist, the contents of which she left for the animals to drink. [Oh, the ingenuity of women!]

We lived in the middle of nowhere – so my mother always had a larder full of tinned food and dry goods. We also had our own chickens and the local farmers had land rovers and tractors to fetch goods, so paradoxically we might have been less affected than the townies. I imagine supplies to shops must have been disrupted. I do remember, or perhaps I may have seen it on the TV News that a coach or bus full of people was stranded at Askerwell, at Askers Roadhouse on the Bridport road which is very high on the downs.

I remember tramping through the snowdrifts the next morning after staying with Liz (who reminded me that the sea did freeze) with Jen from Dorchester to Charminster – roads cut off. Drifts higher than hedges.

I started working in Leeds twenty miles away just in time for the very bad winter of 1963. Trains were regularly stuck outside the station as the points were frozen and it was so cold! Then travelling by car there were snow drifts about four feet high on either side of the road but being in gritty Yorkshire we always made it through! Normal dress for work was either skirts or dresses but during that winter I wore trousers and boots to travel in, changing when arriving at work. We also suffered occasional smoggy days when the best way forward was for the passenger in the car to stick her head out of the window to make sure we were close enough to the side of the road and the driver to try to see the white lines immediately in front.

It went on so long! My beautiful new Mini sat in the garage for three solid months. It was the end of March before I dared to take it out and venture several miles to visit a friend. The moment I turned off the main road on to the one across country, I wished I hadn't! All the snow that had been pushed aside to clear the road had accumulated as huge high banks either side of what amounted to a single carriageway. They dwarfed the Mini; it was like driving through a topless ice tunnel. To this day, I give thanks that no one else was stupid enough to use the road for we would have met head on, there being no space left where it would have been possible to pass. To this day, I can remember the sheer terror of that journey.

The winter of 1963 seemed endless … but I don't remember too much disruption, e.g. schools being closed, lack of public transport etc. Everyone just got on with it. However, I did go on a school trip (a sort of Outward Bound) to Wales in the February. We travelled by train and had real problems with trains taking hours longer than normal. I remember learning to ski, orienteering and having to camp out all night in an old shed/barn. [No wonder our now mature ladies are so resilient if that is an example of a 1960s teenager. Would today's health and safety and risk assessment rules have allowed such a school trip to be undertaken?]

There is no doubt that all these comments prove just how important the weather is to the British!

The Assassination of President Kennedy, 22 November 1963

It is another of those myths that we all remember where we were and what we were doing when we heard the news of the shooting of President Kennedy. Surprisingly there were fewer recollections than expected.

I, like the rest of the population remember exactly what I was doing when we heard of the assassination and the general shock of it. It didn't change my life but one felt for the people of the USA. [It's a pity she did not share her whereabouts.]

I had been to Guides, coming home on my bike about 9 p.m. to find my mother in tears as she watched our small black and white TV. My father worked away from home and my young brother was asleep. We watched together for a while and then I went to bed.

I was sitting in a school-room [at Boarding School] doing my prep when somebody came down all the classrooms to tell us all – horrible time.

I was in London at the time and all the radios were turned up in the shops reporting that he had been shot.

I was at my son's school Open Evening when I heard the news.

As I did most evenings, I was exercising my red pen over a pile of essays. In those days if you taught English in a Grammar School, every class you taught had at least one essay a week that required detailed marking. I was alone in the house, the radio in the background for company, when the news came on. I can remember turning very cold and desperately wanting to talk to someone – but we didn't have a phone, neither did most of my friends. The cat must have picked up my feelings for he suddenly appeared, jumped on my lap, as if to say, 'Well at least I'm here'. I didn't finish my marking that night.

I am one of those who can recall what I was doing when the death of JFK was announced – revising for an exam which would involve questions on the American electoral system.

* * *

In 1966, England's football team captained by Bobby Moore won the World Cup. I watched it in a hotel lounge in King's Lynn, and it seemed as though the whole country was cheering.

Quite a lot was expected of me in terms of helping at home – I can recall mowing the lawn when England won the World Cup in 1966.

Everyone remembers when Sandie Shaw won the Eurovision Song Contest in **1967**.

The Arab-Israeli War, 1967 and the Invasion of Czechoslovakia, 1968

This short-lived war seems to have taken people by surprise. The unexpectedness of it was all the more frightening.

The Arab-Israeli war terrified me. I read some Brian Glanville books at this time, which helped me understand what was going on in the Middle East.

I remember the Soviet invasion of Czechoslovakia in August **1968**. My husband and I belonged to a Czech dance group. Some Czechs were stranded in London and with our landlady's permission we got in touch with the Czech embassy and had an eighteen-year-old student to stay (we had a sofa bed in our living room). He stayed the summer doing some building work in the black economy then returned to Prague at the end of the summer. We later stayed with his family in Prague and still keep in touch.

The Vietnam War, 1957–1969

Though Britain was not officially engaged in the struggle between the north and south of Vietnam, newsreels of the heavy fighting appeared regularly in the cinema and on television.

My concerns at the time were soldiers being sent off to war, and all the starvation in the world, which is still really bad. The Vietnam War was so tragic, such a lot of lives lost or ruined with injuries. I can't believe all the wars that are going on today.

The student uprisings in Paris in early **1968** were of some concern to me as I was just about to begin student life myself. Vietnam, Northern Ireland and the Ugandan Asian crisis were all of concern during student days.

Trouble in Northern Ireland

I was due to join a group of people travelling to Ireland for a holiday. The organisers wrote informing us that 'because there were some local difficulties amongst the people of Northern Ireland' they were making plans to alter the route we were to take if necessary. 'However', they continued, 'the holiday is not due to commence for another eight weeks so it is expected that it will all be sorted out by then.' No harm in hoping, one is forced to comment.

The trouble in Northern Ireland was always a concern to me as I have a few friends that I nursed with who had families in Ireland. It seemed somehow closer to us than all the other trouble spots.

Walking on the Moon, 1969

The American Space Programme had become part of our consciousness from the late 1950s but the culmination for most ordinary people was being able to watch on television as a man actually got out of a spacecraft and walked on the moon. Most mothers tried to communicate to their children just how momentous this was.

We sat up most of the night watching the moon landing, being very excited by it all. I've still got all the newspaper cuttings … we were so proud.

The space project was brilliant and I can remember holding my son up at the window telling him that there was a man on the moon. He waved and said hello to him.

Without a television I missed seeing the astronauts land on the moon but (living in Wales) I could not avoid the Investiture of the Prince of Wales on 1 July, 1969. Two of our neighbours were folk singers and guitarists, and a piano was hauled on to the foundations of one of the unfinished houses, along with spare wood for a big bonfire and logs to sit on. We celebrated loudly and well.

* * *

Contributors were asked for their reaction to the Feminist Movement.

I was well aware of the feminist movement but felt it was a bit OTT as my husband was very fair and we shared everything and there was no inequality in our lifestyle.

I was definitely aware of the feminist movement. I felt privileged to work with the first female camera person at Granada TV (who were way ahead of the BBC in these matters by the way.) I took the magazine *Spare Rib* on a regular basis – and burned my bra – mainly because I did not have much use for it!'

I supported this by my actions – I chose a University course that was normally considered to be for men only and blazed a trail showing that girls were just as able to do engineering subjects as boys if they wished to. I didn't experience any prejudice apart from sneering remarks from my organic chemistry lecturer in Year 1. He changed his tune once I passed his exam!

I never really fancied burning my bra.

I was very much aware of the feminist movement and approved wholeheartedly at first but I came to dislike intensely the brash, aggressive spokeswomen who took it to unrealistic man-hating lengths. The balance between the sexes certainly needed to be evened up but not tipped completely the other way.

I never felt the need for the feminist movement as I always thought I had enough independence and I didn't feel the necessity to burn my bra!

Chapter Seven

Women's Liberation!

Ask any woman under forty-five in the 1960s what was the one thing that made her feel liberated and you will probably be surprised at the answer. It was not that defining moment when she decided to forget all her mother's dire warnings and cast aside her vest in winter. Nor was it the acquisition of a washing machine and tumble-drier, which made washday less of a momentous chore. Neither was it the chest deep freezer stored in a hastily-built lean-to on the back of the kitchen which opened up a whole new world of cookery and neither, oddly enough, was it the availability of the contraceptive pill. No. It was the car! Time and again, women have recalled that it was learning to drive, passing that dreaded test and having ready access to a car that gave them a sense that at last they had achieved independence. No longer reliant on or beholden to father, boyfriend or husband to drop them off at work or the bus stop, pick them up after an evening out or even just take them shopping, they could, at last, finally, go where they wanted, when they wanted, without having to ask anybody else.

Well, more or less that is, in some cases. Take M.O.'s experience for instance. In 1962 she and her husband managed to buy a second-hand car; M.O. was still earning a good wage so she was able to help not only with the car purchase but also to pay for her driving lessons. At the time she stood out, being the only woman in her circle of friends who could drive but it was an ability she rarely had chance to use often, as her husband needed the car to drive to work. Would twenty-first century women have put up with her situation? 'If I wanted the car I had to catch a bus into town, use the car and then return it to the car park so he could drive home later.' The obvious question why did she not wait with the car and they drive home together, can probably be answered by suggesting that she had to precede him home because being very much a 1960s husband, he would have expected a meal on the table when he returned.

Growing up in the Fifties and Sixties most girls depended on their bicycles, not just for pleasure or as a way of keeping up social contacts, but more seriously to get them to school and later to their workplace, though it is doubtful that many can claim, as J.T. does, that she got her place at university on the strength of a bicycle: 'I had a good bicycle – a man's Claud Butler with ten gears and I cycled everywhere. This bicycle secured my place at University as the interviewer was impressed with the fact that I had stripped it down, repainted it and rebuilt it.'

The very fact that J.T. actually managed to get an interview to study for a degree in Industrial Chemistry was in itself surprising at that time, but that she was able to demonstrate that she really had both hands-on as well as theoretical knowledge must surely have impressed even the most sceptical male interviewer.

Those old black-and-white newsreel pictures of the Fifties trotted out to provide atmosphere for period dramas are likely to show workers pouring out through the factory gates, the majority on bikes. A new factory site would include plenty of space for cycle sheds to accommodate the needs of the workforce while close to the main building would be a small parking area for visitors – and management. As far as car ownership went, there was still a great class distinction between them and us – management and workers. Only the wealthy and those whose business depended on their ability to travel distances would have a car and for the latter the car was rarely used for personal purposes. But the Sixties changed all that; suddenly car ownership came within the reach of many in the workforce, not least because the increased production of new cars meant that suddenly there were reasonably-priced second-hand vehicles for sale. This was something that had obviously not been foreseen by the town and city planners responsible for housing estates since they continued to build row upon row of semi-detached houses without either garages or the space to park a car between the houses. By the time the next generation of planners caught up and provided the single garage, such had been the change in family habits that not only double garages were needed but often space too for a third car.

Of course there had always been the motorcycle for those who craved more speed than the pedal cycle would allow and as early as the 1920s young men were taking their girlfriends to the seaside as pillion passengers. The family man, on the other hand, would save up and add a sidecar capable of carrying his wife and possibly two very small children to his sturdy motorcycle. These vehicles, although used by the military to great advantage during the Second World War, fell out of general favour during the 1950s, especially with the young, when they were replaced towards the end of the decade by the Italian-manufactured Vespa and Lambretta scooters which were quickly adopted not only as an inexpensive means of transport but also as a fashion statement by the group, mainly young men, who became known as Mods. The battles that ensued with their rivals the Rockers, on motorbikes, are well documented and do not really concern us here. The Suez Crisis of 1956 that resulted in petrol rationing helped precipitate on to the market the German-manufactured 'Bubble' cars based on a motorcycle engine. These strange looking little cars were basically two-seaters with a space at the back that could take a small child or a small amount of luggage.

Our earlier contributor, J.T. found that living in London in the first half of the 1960s, she needed something more than a bicycle to get her home to Dorset, especially, as with the approaching end of the steam-train era and Dr Beeching's cuts to the railway system generally, who knew if she would still be able to reach her home by rail. So she 'bought a half-share in a yellow Triumph Tigress scooter with my boyfriend and we motored up to London on it. The wretched thing kept breaking down so we sold it and bought a Honda 90, a little motor bike-cum-scooter'. Her friend L., on the other hand, who had not only had a Vespa scooter in her Sixth Form years but had actually had permission to ride it to school, was now married with a baby son and living on the proverbial shoestring, her husband having just graduated and about to start training in the RAF. 'We had bought a 3-wheeler bubble car to get around, as Alec could drive it on his motorbike licence … We used to drive down to Weymouth with the carrycot in the back and the baby on my lap! Can you imagine that nowadays?' The answer to that is, of course, 'no' but we have to remind ourselves that there was much less traffic on the roads in those days; juggernaut lorries were still to come, as were most dual carriageways and motorways and in any case most cars were incapable of very high speeds.

Many girls like J.T. learnt to drive as soon as they were old enough. While still in the sixth form between 1960–2, she learnt with the RAC Junior Drivers' Scheme in an Austin A40 and passed her test but once qualified, her father would not allow her to use his car. However, several of her friends did have access to cars, mainly old Austin Sevens, in which on Saturdays they used to visit various country pubs in their area. She recalled one girl who got stopped by the police after she had managed to cram most of the hockey team into her car! R., another member of this particular band of schoolgirls, said even though her mother never learnt to drive, it been taken for granted that she would. Unlike J.T.'s father who would not allow her to drive his car, R.,'s father started giving her practice lessons on a disused aerodrome that was full of potholes that were, in her words 'good for practising steering'. Then, when she was seventeen, she took out a provisional licence, which lasted for six months before it needed renewing.

My father taught me and I had some 'finishing off' lessons from a colleague of his in order to undo some of the acquired bad habits. I also had the opportunity to drive long distances as a learner driver on the summer trek to visit an aged grandmother in Norfolk. I think we probably had some tense moments! [Did she panic as someone did the first time they encountered a major roundabout? These were few and very far between in Dorset.] I took my test one afternoon, walking out of school in my school uniform, very nervous, to where the examiner was waiting. I managed to pass despite the busy High Street and the tight squeeze past parked cars. I drove only in university holidays. At one point I had a [holiday] job, which required me to drive a Mini emblazoned with an advertising slogan. At another point I was persuaded to hire a car and drive some friends to Oxford from Birmingham – can't remember why. Having a driving licence then, in the mid-60s was by no means the norm.

But it certainly was useful and if a girl wanted to get ahead in some professions it was essential. Following her marriage, S.T. was informed by the Matron of the hospital where she worked that since she was now living twenty-five miles away, there was no way she could make the journey by rail into work and then do a full day's shift so she must leave. After a break in employment of ten weeks, S.T. found part-time work as a district nurse in her local area.

Eventually this was the start of my thirty-four years' service as a district nurse in the small Lakeland town that became my home. I rode my bike in all weathers (it seemed to rain every day!) around the town for the next eighteen months until at last I passed my driving test. It took me three attempts I was so nervous. I remember the day I was given a County car. It was old and black and felt as if it was about to fall apart (they would never get away with that today) but on both front doors it had the County crest. I was so proud of that. It was still old but soon became a very shiny car! I drove this until we were able to save to buy our own car. That was a split screen Morris Minor which cost us £75.0.0. We had to pay for it in two instalments.

When N. started her career as a nanny to a wealthy family, the chauffeur would usually be available to drive her and her young charges to dancing classes or children's parties in one of the cars belonging to the household. If, however, the chauffeur was needed elsewhere, then taxis had to be arranged for Nanny and the children. By the middle of the 1960s prospective employers expected that Nanny listed a clean driving licence on her CV, though they would not necessarily expect her to provide her own car. One of N.'s later employers paid for her driving lessons, her ability to ferry his children around being of paramount importance. In fact an applicant for a post outside London stood little chance of even being considered if she were unable to drive.

Reading through their experiences of learning to drive, it became apparent that the contributors fell into two groups, those who learnt as soon as they were legally able to do so and those who were more mature when they came to driving. Those in the former group were more likely to have grown up with a car in the family and so knew their way around a vehicle and then had plenty of opportunity to practise, needing only the minimum of professional driving tuition. Women in their mid- to late twenties and older most often came to driving without having had access to a family car, while professional single women were more likely to take driving lessons than their married sisters. Often it was a question of necessity; they needed a reliable form of transport to get them to and from work or they worked away from the family home where there was an ageing parent, and so needed to be able to reach it at weekends, holidays and possible emergencies. Professional women were also more likely to travel for pleasure, so again a car became important. Schoolteacher P. provided a good example. A member of a close-knit family, she had obtained a teaching post close enough for her to go back home at the weekend. She started taking a course of lessons during the week. In those days the official driving schools, of which the British School of Motoring (BSM) was best known, preferred their clients to book a course of ten lessons initially, for which there was a slight reduction but of course that meant having to find a lump sum as opposed to the 25 or 30 shillings per lesson. Some older working-women even took the plunge and purchased a car before they had passed their test. This was M.T.'s case.

I got my first car in 1959. It was a Ford Popular, second-hand and cost £250.0.0. It looked a bit old fashioned even then but I loved it and it was great for the family. I was still teaching in Workington and with the help of Albert, a family friend, I was able to drive back there every Sunday while he taught me to drive on the way – he'd been a driver in the Army during the war – then he drove it back to my home. I took my test in Workington where I had my official driving lessons during that year and passed the second time when my hill starts had improved! It made a great difference not just to my life. We could go to Barrow shopping instead of using the train and it was great being able to get out into the countryside and to explore more of the county. It assisted my younger brother later in his courting and it meant hospital appointments were much easier to keep. In fact it widened our horizons a lot – Millom was a bit cut off in those days.

That theme of widening horizons was echoed time and time again, particularly by unmarried women teachers who often used the school holidays to tour all over the British Isles. M.S. and D.O. were two such who discovered by chance that they were both taking driving lessons and then, coincidentally, both took and passed their test on the same day. With the end of the summer term approaching and neither having booked a holiday, they agreed it would be fun to go touring. So they hired a car and took off from Somerset to tour Wales. The plan was that they would share the driving, changing every twenty miles. However, D.O. added, it seemed that her twenty-mile sessions coincided with the towns (which were rarely bypassed in those days), while M.S. got to do the quiet country lanes. The more intrepid ones often headed for foreign parts. One middle-aged art teacher packed her camper van and regularly drove to Italy or the south of France where she spent her holidays painting. She travelled unaccompanied, never giving a second thought to her personal safety. Another, who passed her test in 1963 and through her father's generosity bought a black Austin with a red roof for £300, says of being able to drive: 'It has made all the difference in the world; it provided so much fun and opened life to all kinds of new opportunities and many travelling adventures across the world – most of Europe, Kenya and South Africa.' B. went to work in Kenya in 1968 where she found the most sensible car to drive there was the resilient little VW Beetle.

The British car industry in the early Sixties was dominated by the Morris, Austin and Ford companies who, realising there was a growing market, produced small cars that were affordable, although it has to be remembered that purchase tax could account for as much as one-third of the price paid for a new car. This accounts for why there was a steady market for second-hand cars. However, just before the Budget of 1962, it was rumoured that purchase tax was due to be reduced on new cars and so it was that for the total sum of £500.0.0. S.M. found herself the proud owner of a brand new Austin Seven Mini, surf blue in colour, 'to match your dress', said the car salesman. Considered as somewhat of a trendsetter by her pupils, she had chosen a car that was not only new to the market, it was quite unlike any car she had ever driven. To start with it was much lower to the ground than the others; it had a transverse engine, the battery was in the boot, its wheels were situated squarely at each corner of the car; it was front-wheel drive and it could turn on the proverbial sixpence. The interior was very different too. The windscreen was a very wide curve, the instrument panel was circular and the start button was on the floor! There were large pockets on the doors which opened by a pull-down 'string'. There were sliding windows operated on a press-button system which made doing the regulation hand signals difficult. The rear window was small and unheated, frequently misting up in rainy weather or freezing in winter. One could buy a sort of plastic double-glazing unit that fitted onto the interior of the rear window. One thing it did have in common with other cars at the time was a central join in the rubber framing the rear window which was a most useful guide to positioning the car alongside the pavement when doing the required reversing round a corner. Idiosyncrasies aside, it was a lovely car to drive. Petrol at the time cost under five shillings a gallon and since the mileage capacity of the engine was such that with the tank almost full with four gallons of fuel, one could do a very long journey for under a pound. S.M. said her car drank more water than it did petrol, especially if she used the very basic heater. It served her well for years before rust finally attacked the bottom of the boot. Now in her eighties, the trend-setting Mini driver has done it again, becoming the part owner of an electric car, this time in a pale sky blue!

Twenty-first-century women drivers still have to learn the Highway Code – and pass a theory test as well as the actual driving test – but driving in the Sixties involved using a car without power steering which made the car seem much heavier and sometimes involved something called double declutching unless one had synchronised gears. A woman who had driven a new Triumph Herald in the mid-1960s was delighted when in the late 1980s her son bought his first car, a very old convertible Triumph that haled from the Sixties. His mother climbed into the driving seat ready to relive her memories and was horror-struck to find how hard it was to manoeuvre, having grown soft over the years of driving modern cars. In retelling that story she was reminded of something that has disappeared entirely but was once a part of every new car's life. In those days it was not uncommon to see a brand-new car on the road with a printed notice in the rear window that read 'Running-in, Please Pass'. Having left the factory, a new engine had to be bedded down and eased into life – a bit like a new-born child going through the weaning process. Until about a thousand miles were registered on the 'clock' the car should not be driven above forty miles an hour. If ignored, the driver could end up with an engine using large quantities of oil.

Sixties women not only learnt to drive and maybe own a car, they also took on the responsibility of the maintenance of the vehicle; not just cleaning and polishing it weekly, inside as well as out, but the more serious business of regularly checking the oil level in the engine, topping up the battery with distilled water and keeping the windscreen-washer bottle filled with diluted washing-up liquid. Some women could even change a punctured tyre if they needed to, while others became well acquainted with their car's idiosyncrasies, knowing exactly where to tap the starter motor when the car refused to budge, or if it was a very old one, using a handle to crank up the engine. They knew exactly what the tyre pressures should be and checked these at the local garage where they bought their petrol. One thing they did not have to do was fill the car with petrol. In those more leisurely days, one drove onto a garage forecourt, which housed one or more petrol pumps, and waited for the attendant, often the garage owner, to approach the driver's window to ask how much fuel was required. While the tank was filling, the attendant would carefully clean the windscreen of the car and then ask if there was anything else needed. He – and it usually was a he – then took the money and returned with the change. By 21st-century standards this appears to be both labour-intensive and time-consuming. Arguably, in practice it was neither but with the coming of motorways, heavy traffic and the building of large petrol stations, the small family garages which offered good service were forced out of business being unable to compete with the cut prices offered by the major oil companies. But in the 1960s Mrs or Miss X and her car forged a personal link with her local garage that was advantageous for both parties.

Nurse S.D. learned to drive at the age of twenty-three when she had finished her midwifery training. Two years later she embarked on further training to become a health visitor. The ability to drive would have been a great asset but as she wrote: 'I had learned to drive in 1962 much to the surprise of many people who still considered it an unnecessary skill for women. Surely we should marry and have a man to drive us!! Many of my school friends still do not drive which, of course is a real disadvantage for them when they become less active or are widowed.' It certainly seems to be the case that it was those who could already drive when they married who were much more likely to insist that they should have use of the car, as one wife said, it seemed ridiculous that their car should spend its day parked at a railway station or office car park.

The car, however, was not the only thing that brought women freedom. The 1960s were a great time for offering educational opportunities to anyone who was willing to take them. This was the period of experiments in the school system with the eventual abolition of most of the grammar schools in favour of large neighbourhood comprehensives, thus putting all the eleven to sixteen-year-old boys and girls in one school. At the same time technical schools were also phased out so that children, particularly boys who had their sights set on becoming draughtsmen or craftsmen, lost out. It is only in recent years that the realisation has come, that in the pursuit of offering all children the chance of an academic education, we have lost the advantage of having well-trained craftsmen – remember the stories which circulated a few years ago that the only qualified plumbers available were those who came from Poland?

This was the era too, when many technical colleges and colleges of further education were granted university status, while up and down the country many new universities were created to cope with the demand for places that was coming from the students in the newly-created sixth-form colleges. Universities were also reporting an increase in the number of applications they received from mature students, men and women who had worked for a number of years and saved enough to support them while they undertook the studies they had been denied in their immediate post-school days. This in turn led to a desire to help those who wanted to study at university level but could not afford to give up their jobs. Thus was born the revolutionary concept of the Open University which allowed people to study at home, assisted by occasional residential weekend tutorial sessions plus a residential study week in the summer. Great use was made of television, BBC 2 giving over certain hours of the day, mainly early morning and late in the evening, to programmes devised and presented by the Open University staff. While these were essential for OU students, many other viewers expanded their knowledge by tuning into these programmes.

For those who had neither the time nor the funds to set out on such dedicated courses, in particular women with a young family, their only chance for further study came through attendance at evening classes, a development of the much earlier night school system. The women who attended these classes, which were usually held in local schools, were likely to be either young mothers who had had a good education and then gone into a satisfying career or those who had left school without any qualifications and taken a job which had provided a wage but little real stimulation. These were the women who realised that once their children were at school, they would probably return to the workplace but not necessarily the one they had left. These were women who, often nursing a long held or thwarted ambition to follow a certain career, realised they would need to pass exams to achieve it. Evening classes provided the opportunity for them, offering O level classes in the basics, maths and English, as well as languages, history and geography. For those hoping to eventually make it to university, there was the opportunity to study to A level. While, for those wishing to broaden their horizons or simply to keep their brains stimulated after a day of household chores and the care of young children without having the pressure of an exam at the end of the year, there were lectures on philosophy, psychology, Chinese, art appreciation, Egyptology, archaeology, anthropology, you name it, a good Local Education Authority would provide it, just as long as they could find a suitable tutor. Then there were all the practical courses, cookery, pottery, ballroom dancing, archery, car maintenance, woodwork, upholstery – again, the list of options was sometimes overpowering. Usually during August, the brochures for the classes commencing in September would appear in various places, in particular libraries, or a list would be published in the local paper, also giving the enrolment dates. Sometimes it was a scramble to get into the class of your choice, as the numbers were limited, conversely, if after three weeks the class had fewer than eight members, it was disbanded, in which case the students were offered a transfer to another class or had their fees refunded.

I had just given up teaching, my old-fashioned husband believing I should concentrate on bringing up the children. I missed it very much. I actually found three small boys under six more difficult than the class of forty-three eight to nine years old that I had left! I intended to return when they started school, but two of the children had health problems and needed quite a lot of care, so I had to wait several years. During this time I discovered the pleasure of Evening Classes at the local College and gained many new skills which I used to supplement our income which was sorely stretched.

Most of the classes R.P. attended at the local Civic College came under the heading of 'Leisure', which for some of them simply meant that there was not an examination at the end of the course. Crafts of all sorts had interested her, and her ability in this sphere had been particularly useful in her teaching. Thinking ahead to the time when she could return to work, and hoping that she might change to secondary pupils, she decided she would develop her already considerable needlework skills, so she did a course in tailoring. All the members of the family were able to benefit from this, as they did from the two-year cookery course that followed. Next came woodcarving, which she loved but getting suitable wood to use proved both difficult and expensive. Pottery followed and then it was back to Art at which she had excelled at school, so she joined an oil-painting class. That, alas, she was unable to pursue, as her husband was allergic to the smell of the oil paint. Instead she honed her skills and learnt new techniques with watercolours. With this she had at last found both the mental stimulation and satisfaction of a relaxing hobby and in time, as her work became recognised, a financially rewarding one.

Many young women, particularly those who were working, perhaps in sedentary jobs, joined classes involving physical activity such as keep-fit, yoga, fencing and badminton. Often two friends would go to a class together and perhaps topped off with a quick cup of coffee in a nearby coffee bar, would look upon the occasion as a 'girls' night out'. However, one of the big attractions to evening classes was that one could go by oneself and invariably, it was not long before one had made friends within the group, some lasting for years. Magazine 'agony aunts' of the period regularly suggested classes as a way to solving their correspondents' problems, whether it be a cure for loneliness for the wife whose husband worked away for home or went out with his friends, or the married woman who had moved into a new neighbourhood. Finally, for the young woman whose work meant she rarely came into contact with men, evening classes were thought to be a sure-fire way of finding a boyfriend, if not a potential husband. Alas, the car maintenance, woodwork, pottery and DIY classes were almost always oversubscribed with women. The men were often to be found in the academic classes, making up for what they had missed at school prior to going on to further education.

And sadly, for the single women, most of the men who did attend classes were married. That is not to say that romance was not to be found in the unlikely venue of a school gymnasium where the badminton was played. Mixed pairs sometimes led to very close friendships developing between partners which could in time become so intense as to lead to the break-up of two marriages,

Towards the end of the decade there seems to have been a surge among women to think about returning to work. It was not just a question of asserting their independence: in many cases, as we shall see later, it was driven by financial necessity. The children who were born at the beginning of the period were now at school, many of them leaving mother free for most of the day. Washing machines and vacuum cleaners had cut down on housework, as their mothers had known it; fridges meant that it was no longer necessary to shop daily for fresh food and cooking was being transformed with the availability of frozen, canned and dried food. So some women found that there was not sufficient to fill their time. M.O., for example, spent long hours gardening and then turning her produce into jams, chutneys, and preserved fruit, but this was not enough to keep her brain occupied.

Once the children started school I decided I would like to return to work. My husband was very much against this as none of his friends' wives worked, but I was bored and money was still tight. I applied for several jobs but was not successful, my qualifications were out of date and employers were loath to take on an employee with two young children. Then I read of a new course starting at the local College entitled 'A Refresher Course for Married Women Wishing to Return to Work'. Apparently there was a great demand for experienced clerical workers and the College was in contact with a lot of local employers. The course was free, held during the afternoon, during the children's school hours and was a refresher course for typing and shorthand, at the end of which we would take the examination with the other College students and hopefully find employment. I enrolled for the class which started in the autumn of 1970!

There was not just a shortage of experienced clerical workers; there was also an acute shortage of both teachers and nurses. As R.P. reported earlier when she gave up teaching in the early part of the Sixties, she had forty-three boys and girls in her class. The school population was still growing; the rising birth rate in the country reaching school age was added to by immigration as D. found when she was given the job of running a language unit in the Bletchley area for children drawn from three schools, infant, junior and secondary. Her pupils included Italians, Sicilians, Indians and Pakistanis with one lone Chinese. To meet the need, teacher training colleges set up emergency courses to train mature women. Realising that their applicants would all have family responsibilities, the courses were non-residential with hours to fit round the school day of the students' own children. In Ipswich, for example, where the nearest training college was Keswick Hall, Norwich, an extension of that college was set up at Belstead House. Similarly, hospitals also opened their doors to mature women to train as nurses. Doors were opening in many professions that would allow women to study and go on to make satisfying careers for life. Women were needed – and unlike wartime when they had taken over the jobs of men and shown they could do them, they were not going to be cast aside when no longer required. Sixties' women forged the way forward that 21st-century women now take for granted.

Yet still, after all these years, the belief persists that it was the contraceptive pill that gave women freedom.

Chapter Eight

Fashion

'You're not going out dressed like that!' How many women can truthfully say that at some point in their teens one of their parents, most likely their father, will have uttered those fateful words. It is likely that the fictional Elizabeth Bennett's father might have bestirred himself to comment thus when he saw that his younger daughters had dampened their muslin gowns in order to make them show off the silhouette of their bodies. No doubt Victorian papas said it to daughters who dared to display an ankle, while 1920s fathers must have taken one look at the flimsy, straight dresses which barely covered the knee and ordered the wearer to her room. In the 1940s and 1950s it was more likely to be heavy make-up that roused parental ire but come the Sixties, so we are led to believe, it was the miniskirt which caused the most agitation, yet as we shall see, that did not really have an impact until at least halfway through the decade.

During the Fifties, fashion was still dictated by what was suitable for the occasion. Young women who worked in schools, shops and offices were expected to look neat and tidy from top to toe; hence the almost uniformity of the suit with its pencil skirt, sparkling white blouse and tailored jacket. For winter wear, particularly in poorly-heated offices, a gored skirt in a woollen material would be paired with jumpers and cardigans, mostly home-knitted. Trousers, of course, were not even considered for the workplace. Overcoats and raincoats at the appropriate times of the year and hats completed the everyday outfit. For special occasions the influence of Jackie Kennedy and Grace Kelly was much in evidence, a little dress topped with a boxy jacket, a pillbox hat and white gloves for the former, a collarless suit with a nipped-in waist, a large dinner plate-sized hat with a down-turned brim and the inevitable short white gloves for the latter. In the 1950s many women wore white gloves in summer and either leather or woollen gloves in winter. Shoes had pointed toes and a medium heel and handbags were often sold in colours and material to match the shoes – and in some shops matching gloves were offered too. American styles as seen worn in films of the period greatly influenced summer dresses in this country. Whether it was a complete frock or a colourful skirt worn with a contrasting colour blouse, both had very full skirts to just below the knee. By the very end of the Fifties, young women were wearing several layers of highly starched petticoats to make their skirts stand out even more.

As we entered the Sixties, the full skirts lingered on for summer wear and Saturday night dances but older girls and the more mature women were then opting for the sleeveless shift dress which started off below the knee but gradually got shorter as the decade progressed. The shift dress was easy to wear and even easier to make; it did not require much material, there were no sleeves to set in or collar to attach, in fact those women who were adept with the sewing machine like F., often went out on Saturday morning, bought the material required, returned home and by the time they left home to go to the local dance hall they were wearing a brand-new dress. M.H., on the other hand, had a mother 'who was a keen seamstress and made most of my clothes. There were occasional nods to modern fashion with my first shift dress and the annual adjustment of hemlines, depending on how far the hemline had crept up or how much I'd grown.'

J.T., who perhaps should have written her own book on the 1960s so clear are her recollections, gave such detailed accounts of the clothes she was wearing that they warrant quoting in full.

1960–1962. I didn't have many clothes and most were hand-made by myself. I did buy a multi-layered can-can petticoat and a lemon yellow blouse with my first wage packet from my holiday job in the kitchen of a seaside restaurant (£2.10s.0d for 6, 8 hour days). We used to soak these nylon petticoats in a sugar solution to stiffen the layers of net. Mum bought me a yellow PVC three-quarter-length coat from Freeman's or Grattan's catalogue. I had to smuggle this in and out of the house, as Dad wasn't to know! I also had a pair of tartan trousers. I made a full skirt from multi-coloured striped Viyella and a long sleeved shirtwaster dress in red Viyella. I have a photograph of myself on the beach wearing a handmade (by me) turquoise terry towelling bikini!

1962–1966. I lived in a pair of black ski pants and a large hand-knitted sky blue jumper during the winter at university. I also had a straight style dark green dress with gold flecks through it for formal dinners. This was bought in a sale at home. In my first year in London, I had a WHITE coat, which promptly got ruined when a vehicle sprayed filthy black water all over me outside the cigarette factory in Mornington Crescent. I cried as it was all I had. My next coat was a black duffle.

1966–1970. I still made most of my clothes and so did my friends. One friend made herself a new dress every Saturday for the evening's parties. A great deal of Sellotape was involved in these creations [unlike F's which were carefully machined]. I made a super pale blue and white cotton trouser and tunic outfit – the back of the tunic had a lot of open space. I also made a very short jump suit from a dark navy fabric with large pink flowers. I loved both these outfits which were accessorised with large plastic flower clip-on earrings. I thought I was 'the bee's knees' in these. Flower Power had arrived! I remember too the buzz that went round Harlow when the new Chelsea Girl shop opened. They sold Afghan coats, which were all the rage. The shop had to close for fumigation the next week due to a severe flea infestation!

It is noticeable that nowhere does J.T. mention the miniskirt, that item which has come to epitomise the 1960s, yet truth to tell these did not appear much outside London until the middle of the decade. However, J.K., who was J.T.'s contemporary at school, mentions that she wore both miniskirts and hot pants from about 1967. Another young woman working in London said: 'We all fell under the spell of the miniskirt. Anybody young enough to get away with it, wore one.' And there's the rub as two other contributors wrote tersely, 'I did not have the legs for a miniskirt'. 'I did make one excursion into miniskirts, instantly realised that I lacked the legs for such clothing and have avoided the fashion each time it has returned since.' On the other hand, M.O. still remembers her first mini-dress:

> It was red and I made it myself. Unfortunately I could not afford any tights to wear with it, as they were very expensive, so I wore this dress with ordinary stockings and suspenders. This was fine whilst standing or walking but as soon as I sat down much to my dismay my suspenders were on display and I spent a lot of time pulling the hem down. I very quickly bought a pair of tights before I wore the dress again.

M.O. was luckier than S.T. who complained that every time she wore a miniskirt or dress her mother would pull the hem down and whenever her mother saw a girl in a really short skirt, she would say, 'if that skirt was any shorter it would be a cummerbund'. A recent pundit describing the morals of the 1960s maintained that the miniskirt was an encouragement to young men towards more direct sexual advances. This seems rather dubious: in fact it could be said the opposite was true. Once tights became fashionable and then cheaper, the naive young man was no longer inflamed by the sight and/ or touch of a suspender and stockings, which might eventually be removed; instead he was now met with a complicated nylon maze.

Like J.T., W. has vivid recollections of the clothes she wore during the Sixties, influenced by her strong interest in fashion and design and a mother who had trained as a court dressmaker. While some of W.'s descriptions will revive memories for some, younger readers will no doubt be surprised to discover that what they had thought were recent trends have all happened before.

In the local shopping centre [1963] there was a small fashionable dress shop and I looked to the window display to guide my taste. On one occasion the mannequin wore a shirt in narrow black striped cotton, a mustard coloured tie and a brown suede jerkin with slit pockets on the hips. I wanted it – badly. The shirt was not a problem, but the jerkin was simply out of my reach. However, my mother had been given some remnants from a handbag factory and had some pieces of brown leather which, reversed, produced the required suede. With my dog-tooth check pleated skirt I wore this outfit all the time.

My winter coat was made from peatbrown/black knobbly Donegal tweed. It was double breasted in the military style with black suede buttons and a teal blue lining. When I received my school certificates I wore a navy blue wool crepe dress. It was 'A' line, had a round neck and long tight sleeves with a circular frill at the wrist.

Around this time [1965] the 1920s and 30s influenced much design. I had a pair of carnation coloured shoes with a bar over the instep and a low curvy heel. I remember wearing a wine coloured kilt which I once absent-mindedly used as a paint rag. I had a black polo-neck jumper – for many years! A number of us wore duffles in winter and I had been given a brown fur helmet which clipped under the chin. I also had an Ungaro-inspired woollen dress. The basic dress was beige; it had a broad black cross across the chest and down the front. On one shoulder there was a purple square. A summer dress, which I wore to college, was a tent shape with a zip down to the waist with a ring pull. It was made from muted lime green canvas-like cotton, had a stand up collar and long flared sleeved.

It is probably true that it was only in the Sixties that clothes were made specifically for young people; until then manufacturers had produced styles for a standard size (W and WX) which could be worn by twenty-year-old women to those of forty and fifty. However, any one having a bust measurement of 40 inches or more was promptly labelled 'outsize' (OS) and regardless of age had little choice of anything that did not have a cross over bodice, muted colours and was deliberately styled 'for the older woman'. Some shops did not stock any large sizes while others had a separate department with the words 'Outsize Dept' prominently displayed. There was nothing so demoralising for the larger young woman as having a svelte, beautifully-groomed, superior-looking shop assistant slowly looking her up and down and then hearing those chilling words, 'I'm afraid we have nothing in your size, Madam', knowing full well she was not a bit sorry. Under the circumstances it is not surprising that so many women, who were able to lay their hands on a sewing machine (usually a Singer), made their own clothes. That way they could adapt a pattern to fit them and they did not need to look older than they were. DS, however, describes the other extreme.

I used to 'knock up' miniskirts out of a yard [36in /91cm] of material – my Needlework teacher would have been horrified. I was 34in round the hip and the material was 36in wide, leaving 2in for the seam and the insertion of a zip (often taken out of a skirt I no longer liked.) Most of the clothes I bought came from children's departments. Until Biba arrived in the King's Road [Chelsea], it was impossible to buy an evening frock or a suit or coat if you were small. Even Marks and Spencer didn't sell clothes (or bras!) smaller than 36in bust. It wasn't until I worked in repertory, where the wardrobe mistress had to make a set of patterns for me, that I could wear fashionable clothes. My parents gave me a second-hand sewing machine for my twenty-first birthday and I was then able to run up frocks – mainly shifts– whenever I wanted. Most of the time I wore jeans anyway

There could be quite serious drawbacks to wearing the miniskirt, however, as student nurse H.P. testified.

In Cambridge in 1968 we all wore miniskirts, as short as possible [when off duty]. I got a kidney infection sitting on a bridge in winter with only a pair of pants and tights between me and the damp stone. Next day, in hospital for a week! We wore a pair of knickers under our tights and another over the top of the tights.

On the other hand, less serious but hard to bear were the results recorded by D during her time at a mixed teacher training college: 'Miniskirts arrived in Oxford in 1965, and those of us in the second year without them suddenly found ourselves minus the boyfriends we'd thought ours for life! However, we managed to bring ourselves up to date and balance was regained.'

On the subject of underwear, it may come as a surprise to discover that a 1964 craft magazine included a pattern for cami-knickers, those wide-legged, gusset-fastened creations which, made of rayon or satin, were very popular in the 1940s. These, however, were knitted in fine two-ply wool. Knitted vests were quite common at one time but knitted knickers? While being somewhat strange, to say the least, had H.P. been wearing a pair of these under her tights she might have been spared her stay in hospital!

In the Sixties, Saturday afternoon shopping for pleasure was almost a ritual. This was an opportunity to look in shop windows and dream or go round the large chain stores to look at clothes or even try some on. Although younger women did not wear hats every day as their mothers still did, that did not stop them from trying them on in Marks and Spencer, British Home Stores and Littlewoods, all of whom set out a generous selection of their stock and provided mirrors so that one could decide which particular style suited one. On a wet Saturday afternoon one could easily pass half an hour in the dry trying on hats. This was more difficult in the large department stores where eagle-eyed assistants soon weighed up the potential customer from the time-waster. For those in London it was rather different. H. and T. both recalled:

When I started work in the bank in London, in my lunch break I would go into the West End to buy clothes and shoes. I loved Mary Quant's clothes and make up. I spent time going to shops like Biba and Bus Stop in the King's Road and also Carnaby Street. I was lucky as my Mum loved all the latest fashions and encouraged my taste in clothes but a lot of my friends were not allowed to wear modern clothes so they used to hide them from their parents and only put them on outside the house.

[As J.T. did with her yellow PVC coat. In her case it would appear to have been that her father disapproved of her mother buying the coat for her from a catalogue, rather than disapproval of the fashion.]

Most of my shopping was done in Colchester but we also went up to London quite often on a Saturday. I know I spent a lot of time (and money) in Carnaby Street and Biba. I wish I'd kept some of the clothes, especially Biba's – they're worth a fortune now.

B.R. reminds us that around 1962 when she worked in the make-up department of a high-class provincial department store, she got the opportunity to go to London for training by Elizabeth Arden. Dance was her great love and she took lessons in all types, ballet, ballroom and jazz. Thus it was her good deportment as well as her expert make-up that led to her being selected as a model for the fashion shows that the store staged two or three times a year. In those far-off days, interested lady customers would take their seats in the restaurant and while they drank their coffee or afternoon tea, the chosen assistants would parade between the tables, perhaps dreaming, as they showed off the latest clothes of the season, that one day they would become as famous as the model Jean Shrimpton (Twiggy was to come later).

For some young women, Mary Quant appealed to all aspects of fashion, said R:

With the deep fringe, dark rimmed eyes, very short skirts and 'bar' shoes with chunky heels – and little white boots. With my first university grant cheque I went into Birmingham to buy a pair of little white boots from Dolcis – or somewhere fashionable. It was the famous freezing cold winter of 1962–63, and my new purchase quickly fell to pieces! And they were freezing cold into the bargain. Arriving home for the first Christmas holiday, I was quickly taken to a sensible shoe shop to buy a sturdy pair of suede ankle boots with thick rubber soles, which would last forever (they resided in the children's dressing-up box for ages). They were indestructible and perfect for the months of snow and frozen slush that winter. My other life saver was a three-quarter length sheepskin coat bought from a saddler's shop. My fellow students in Birmingham actually admired it, and I had offers to buy it! It was the only thing that kept me warm at bus stops in the freezing fog of that winter – when the smog actually permeated one's room.

Most high streets had had two or three shops devoted to the sale of shoes. For everyday, sensible, affordable shoes one would visit one of the chains such as Bata, Stead and Simpson and Freeman, Hardy and Willis. Then there were the independently-owned shops, which specialised in the more expensive fashion shoes from well-known British manufacturers. These shops tended to have well-defined departments to cater for every member of the family. Here one brought the newly-walking infant to be fitted for his or her first shoes. Care was taken as the child grew that shoes were properly fitted, not to big, not too tight and should the child be showing signs of becoming pigeon-toed or wearing down a heel too much, then the well-trained assistant was on hand to give advice to the mother. For the child, for whom 'new shoes' were always exciting, many of these shops had a large rocking horse in the children's department upon which they were allowed to climb. Years later 'battles' would be fought over the choice wished for by the adolescent child. Mother, backed up by school regulations, usually won the day. But here again, the 1960s brought change with the arrival of the chains like Dolcis who aimed to attract the younger, fashion-conscious woman. Forget the sensible black, brown or navy blue court shoes with the two-inch heels, discreetly displayed: here were to be found bright glossy red, green, blue and even yellow shoes with pointed toes and tiny heels which could be matched up with handbags in assorted shapes – and all at an affordable price. It was now possible to have more than a pair for work and another for Sunday; one could match one's shoes to one's outfits and have several changes. Then came the stiletto heels, which wreaked such damage to floors and caused women's feet to become squeezed into the narrow pointed toe. Oh, they were lovely! But many 1960s women can bear testimony now to the legacy of twisted toes.

While the mini and other young fashions were all the rage in the 'with-it' shops in London, the other fashion most copied by teenagers and young women in their twenties and possibly early thirties was the hairstyle created by Vidal Sassoon. According to P.H., 'he took London by storm and I remember spending a fortune and enduring a painful time when I had my hair straightened to keep up with his Mary Quant straight geometrical style. Not prepared to repeat the performance, I then had my hair cut to half an inch all over.'

Those who were not around in the 1960s may well get the impression from the mythology that surrounds the era that hairstyles as such had not existed until then. Quite apart from the roaring trade that was done during the 1950s with home perms, many different styles were by then being demonstrated on television by Raymond, 'Mr Teasy Weasy'. He it was, who employed Sassoon and taught him that the basis of any good hairstyle lay in the cutting. Raymond favoured the use of colour and sleek lines, preferable keeping the hair short. He believed that no one over the age of twenty should wear their hair long as he considered that was ageing. Vidal Sassoon took what he had learned by reinventing the classic bob, turning it into a geometric 'masterpiece' or so his many fans thought.

It would seem that it was mainly unmarried, working women living in London who visited the great man's salon. 'I remember treating myself to have my hair cut at Vidal Sassoon when I lived in London. I think it cost £20, which was a lot of money in 1968.' [It certainly was! Probably a week's salary.] J.K. was luckier, she also had her hair cut at Vidal Sassoon's but she got it free as an apprentice did it! D.S., who had waist-length hair, which she did not wish to cut, was able to follow fashion with the compromise of a red Vidal Sassoon wig.

Those who did not get to experience the London salon but relied on their local hairdresser or perhaps a friend, talk not so much of Sassoon as of having a 'Twiggy' haircut. S.T. recorded that 'at one point in the Sixties I did have a "Twiggy" cut, very short and close to the head, cut by my sister-in-law'. On the other hand, R. remembered having a Cilla Black hairstyle, long at the sides and short at the back. But for the rest of the women throughout the country, just as now, they continued with their weekly shampoo-and-set or cut and blow-dry at the establishment that was most convenient for them. Here, over the years, they made friends with the lady owner and their chosen stylist and if they had a regular appointment on a certain day of the week, they also made a whole new circle of acquaintances with whom they could not only discuss the topics of the day, but also share in the ups and downs of their lives. Regulars also watched the Saturday girl rise through the ranks from sweeping the floor to shampooing and after attendance at hairdressing college becoming fully fledged in such arts as razor cutting, permanent waving, dyeing and back combing. Was it the antidote to Sassoon's geometric style that brought on the bouffant? Some women, particularly those with long hair, had so much backcombing that they developed what became known as the 'beehive style,' while others were content to settle for what can only be described as the cottage loaf! Some of these styles required so much lacquer that it was reported that one girl nearly set her head alight when she came too close to a Bunsen burner in a laboratory. This was the time too, when the more daring were choosing hair dyes, not just all-over colour but streaks, usually blonde ones, but the younger, more daring women might even opt for pink or purple. The cases of schoolgirls turning up to school on a Monday morning with green hair were fairly rare but certainly not isolated; they had found to their dismay that home hair-dyeing was not as easy as they thought!

It is usually clothes that come to mind when we hear the word fashion, so having disposed of the miniskirt and dress, let us consider what most women were wearing. As with a guide to what people were eating, two magazines of the period, *Everywoman* for September 1964 and *Woman and Home* for April 1969 should give an indication of what had happened in the world of fashion throughout most of the Sixties. Two things stand out; the first is that home knitted garments were still very much in evidence and the second that for the women who didn't knit, even with the aid of a knitting machine, many more of them were sewing instead. Although shops were full of ready-to-wear clothes, they were still relatively expensive, so it was partly economics which led many to join the make-it-yourself brigade. During the 1950s and 1960s the woollen mills were producing knitting wool that was no longer just pure wool but mixtures with different textures and additives which would overcome the necessity to wash the garment with great care in order to prevent that greatest of fears, shrinkage. Pure wool required hand washing with the gentlest of soap flakes and then after rinsing and perhaps rolling in a towel in order to remove excess water, had to be laid out somewhere flat to dry. Manufacturers soon came up with a framework containing narrow nylon-covered bars that could be placed across the bath for this purpose. But drying pure woollen garments was always a problem, even more so when the garment was a large one. This helps to explain why in the 1960s so many thick jumpers and cardigans worn by men were not washed as often as they should have been. (Not helped either because at that time few men used anti-perspirants or deodorants!) Furthermore, once most housewives had a washing machine they did not want to have to hand-wash items as well. So we find advertisements for 'Bri-nylon' knitwear, for example, which promised that garments made from it would keep their shape, would not pill or fluff and, best of all, were machine-washable.

In 1964 there was a pattern for a knitted suit using Crepe wool. It consisted of a long line jumper and a pleated skirt. It was advertised as being suitable for any age and used, 'a new idea – the jersey and skirt are held in one with Velcro'. How committed – and competent – one had to be to contemplate this project (and by today's standards how much would the wool cost) since for the three sizes given, the jumper took between fifteen to seventeen ounces and the skirt sixteen to twenty? The jumper had the dropped waistline to just above the hips that was much in evidence both for knitted and ready-made material outfits. While the swirls of pleats set into a lowered waistband 'spell flattery to those with a not so slim waist'. How disappointing, if one was a slavish follower of fashion, to have spent hours making this outfit because, for the autumn of that year, the new silhouette was the slim, high-waisted Empire line. The dropped waist had moved upwards, from the hips up to just under the bust. For the not so slim was the shirtwaster and best of all was the shift, providing it was not too figure-hugging.

By April 1969 *Woman and Home* offered a selection of summer outfits. The hemline had settled at the knee, sleeveless shift dresses were teamed with matching coats, double or single breasted with a slight flair from the waist. Hats were still considered part of the ensemble, younger women wearing little straw boaters with red, white and blue bands to match the same colours in an almost 1950s style dress with a short box jacket. The dress and jacket featured for the more mature woman had 'the added bonus of being up to 42 in. hip'. Shoes had reverted from stiletto heels back to sensible courts with 1¼in heels, or flats. Jersey and Moygashel were much used as was boucle but the newcomer on the scene was 'the linen-look Crimplene', which would become the material of the 1970s.

Given that by 1969 there was much talk of the feminist movement and the campaign to 'burn your bra!' it was surprising the find that there was quite heavy advertising for corselettes and other control garments. For years small, discreet shops selling corsets, brassieres and other lingerie items had been part of every town's shopping area. Here ladies could be fitted with the control garments most suitable for their figures. The corsets which covered the waist to the top of the thighs usually features metal hook and eye fasteners either to one side or right down the front while either at the back or to one side was a panel covered with criss-crossed lacing which allowed the wearer to tighten or loosen according to the current state of her figure. Attached at the thigh area were the suspenders that fastened on to the wearer's stockings. Even in the 1960s mothers were likely to put their teenage daughters into what was colloquially known as 'armour plating'. For women who required a sleek silhouette, particularly under an evening dress, then the all-in-one corselette was the answer. These could vary in the strength of control they offered. Brassieres, as they were still called, also came in different shapes and control but in the 1960s the emphasis was still on uplift. For those who preferred even more personal service, then they could call upon a Spirella consultant, a trained corsetier who would come to a client's home to advise on style and then take measurements which were then sent off to be made at the Spirella factory. However, the personal services offered by both the little shop, usually trading under Madame Isabella or Alberta or some such reassuring name, and the Spirella consultant came at a price and they were both hit hard in the later part of the decade by competition not only by the big manufacturers like Gossard and Berlei but by the own brands of Marks and Spencer and other large stores. Although they all offered their customers an in-store fitting service, most of the younger women simply bought over the counter, much to their mothers' chagrin.

Did the Sixties' women worry about their figures and their size? Silly question! Have women ever been entirely satisfied with the bodies they have been given? There were always one or two girls in every class at school who was bigger than the rest, the ones who were described as having puppy fat, which, so their mothers hoped, would disappear as they grew up. The overweight young woman might consult her doctor who was likely to put her on to thyroid tablets, just in case it was a glandular problem. When that made no difference, the patient was advised to cut out carbohydrates; bread, potatoes, cakes and biscuits and substituting Ryvita or Energen Rolls for bread. Occasionally one of the women's magazines would offer a helpful slimming diet, usually based on the much earlier Hay diet used by the upper classes and celebrities who could afford to spend a week at a health farm. What were also to be found in the magazines were the advertisements for slimming aids in the form of vegetable or herbal-based tablets. There were even two products which came in the form of a caramel-type sweet to be chewed before eating each meal. Pure lemon juice, marketed as PLJ, was also recommended as a slimming aid as were Bisks, and Harley Discs, the latter, available by mail order, were advertised as resulting in a loss of a stone and a half in five weeks. The first slimming club was started by a small group of women at the end of 1969 but occasionally magazines would offer advice on exercise to tone up the body. Just as the twenty-first century has a problem with obesity, it also retains a perennial problem that beset women in the 1960s just as it had for generations earlier. The 1960s' magazines were full of discreet advertisements for dealing with the removal of facial hair. These ranged from pumice-like disks to rub over lip and chin, through various 'miracle' creams and little pots of heated wax to expensive electrolysis.

With the increase in those wearing tights as opposed to stockings, there was no longer a need for suspenders attached to a corset. And for those who needed tummy flattening came the panty girdle and then control briefs of various strength, all of which was possible through the development of new materials. Then, just as vests began to disappear, except in very cold weather, so too did knickers – not the original garment itself but the name – women no longer wore knickers, they wore briefs, and indeed some of them were very brief indeed. Pants or panties enjoyed their turn to describe this essential garment but we have come full circle when suddenly knickers made a return, first to describe the male undergarment, but now reclaimed by females.

For those women who enjoyed sewing but were not happy to make a garment entirely from scratch, most women's magazines would regularly offer 'cut-out-ready-to-sew garments'. From simple summer dresses, two piece suits, right through to a matching winter dress and coat, great was the excitement when the parcel arrived complete with zips and matching buttons as well as foolproof instructions on how to put it together. A new outfit could be had for less than half the price of one in the shop, often costing as little as £3.0.0. or its equivalent in shillings (60/-). For non-knitters and 'dressmakingphobics', there was another way to obtain ready-made clothes without visiting a shop and that was by using one of the large catalogue firms. Twenty-first century women take it for granted that they can now 'go on line' and search the many firms offering stylish clothes in sizes that were once unheard of. With the press of a few keys they can have an entire wardrobe (should they so wish) delivered to their home in a few days. If they still enjoy the experience of going into a store, then they can do that, select the item they want and then go home and order from the Internet. The 1960s version of this was to look in one of the huge mail-order catalogues such as Grattan's, Freeman's, Kays or Littlewoods. These firms provided practically every item anyone could need from a set of saucepans to a man's new suit. The colourful pages brought style and glamour with film-star type models wearing clothes that could be yours for only a few shillings each week.

Opinion was divided on the use of catalogues. There were those who thought it wrong to encourage women to buy items they could not afford by offering to let them pay in instalments. On the other hand, if it helped to spread the cost of a pair of shoes for a child or a new winter coat without running too deeply into the family finances – who could argue with that? In addition, acting as an agent and running a catalogue or even two was one of the few opportunities the stay-at-home mother had to earn some money that she could use for herself or to make a very welcome addition to family finances. D.T., whose son spent many years of treatment that involved lengthy stays in the Children's Hospital in Great Ormond Street, ran both Grattan's and Freeman's catalogues from her home to make money to help pay for the family's weekend expenses and coach fares (cheaper than by train although much longer) to London and back. The two she was involved with must have been among the most popular companies as J.T.'s yellow PVC coat mentioned earlier came from the same source.

Those like the women who have shared their memories and have seen fashions change, will have decided long ago what suits them best and will no doubt agree with the one who said of the miniskirt that it was a fashion she avoided 'each time it returned' because, of course, fashions come and go – and then come back again. Many may think it is a pity we ever discarded our old clothes. If we had not, then every few years or so we could simply recycle them – or should that be 'up-cycle?' –since the word 'recycle' has now been recycled too!

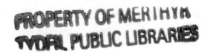

Chapter Nine

Leisure

It looked like being the worst day of our lives. Four weeks to our wedding and we still hadn't found anywhere to live in this unfamiliar town where in six weeks one of us was due to start a new job. We both lived many miles away and had only the weekends for our search, which so far had been unsuccessful. On this particular Saturday, as a result of an advertisement in the local newspaper, we'd come armed with appointments to view three possibilities. The first two offered furnished rooms in old Edwardian houses both of which had indoor plumbing on the ground floor, off the kitchen which we would be expected to share, while the rooms for rent were upstairs. The first was awful so we made our excuses and left. The second was not ideal but possible. We explained to the landlady that we had another appointment but we would be back at 6 p.m. to give her our answer. We were pinning our hopes on what was described as a garden flat – a flat that had its own entrance, a kitchen and a bathroom. We were interviewed by the owners, two elderly ladies who lived in the house next door. That encounter was an experience in itself. It was like stepping into a film set, not quite Miss Havisham's house in *Great Expectations*, more *Arsenic and Old Lace*. The sitting room was full of furniture that their father must have brought back from India in the 1920s or perhaps earlier. We passed the interview, although one of the ladies did bemoan the fact that my fiancé was not a curate! Apparently they had set their hearts on such a tenant. Eventually we were told we might go and see the flat. The moment the current tenants opened the door we knew it was not for us. The place smelt of damp and we quickly saw that in some rooms not only was the wallpaper peeling off the wall, you could actually see huge damp patches and thick mould. The whole place needed condemning. The couple living there were desperate to be re-housed; they had two small children one of whom had become a severe asthmatic. We couldn't get out fast enough. So, it was back to the second set of rooms we had seen. As we approached the front door, we could see a piece of paper was stuck to the knocker. It read 'I have let the rooms to someone else'. What to do now? Despair, disappointment, frustration followed and then the sudden realisation we were both hungry – we hadn't eaten all day. An hour later everything looked better and we were ready to face the world again – we had found a Berni Inn.

The significance of that lengthy account, which incidentally highlights the problem of accommodation that was still common in 1965, lies in the last phrase. Berni Inns played a part in the lives of most 1960s women, especially those living outside London, as the American-inspired steak bars opened in most of the larger towns. Now free of the restrictions on food of the post-war period and influenced by life as depicted in American films – 'May I take you to dinner?' was a question that featured large in them – young couples in particular were beginning to treat a meal out as an occasion in itself rather than a necessity before or after a visit to the theatre or cinema. For years, many had believed that eating in a restaurant was not for the likes of them, that it was a middle- or upper-class prerogative and to some extent this was true if the restaurant was an expensive one. Lyons teashops and restaurants had catered for those whose means were limited but who occasionally longed for a bit of 'class' that was found especially in one of their Corner Houses where the tables were properly laid with silverware on white cloths, with service by correctly-attired waitresses and even, at times, the accompaniment of a trio or quartet gently playing in the background. Additionally, Lyons was one of the few places a woman could go to eat on her own or with a girl friend without question or, as happened sometimes in hotel restaurants, finding herself seated at a very small table close to the kitchen.

Berni Inns were different. Although decked out in mock-Tudor style they were demonstrably modern. In the early days they offered a half-pound Argentine steak, chips and peas, followed by either a miniature block of ice cream of the sort normally served between two wafers or a small piece of Cheddar cheese and two cream crackers, all for seven shillings and sixpence (37½p) per head. Later they expanded their menu to include gammon steak and plaice and chips, a prawn cocktail starter and the ubiquitous Black Forest gateau for dessert and later still they added a salad bar. Interestingly, Berni Inns were instrumental in introducing a whole new generation to sherry. Traditionally drunk as an aperitif by the upper classes, and as a drink for the ladies at Christmas, with their tie up with Harveys, the wine merchants of Bristol, the steak houses offered a choice of a Fino at 3/8d or Bristol Cream at 3/5d for a schooner – which was larger than the normal glass sold for 2/5d or 2/3d – as a pre-meal drink. But the icing on the cake for our accommodation – seekers on that fateful night was when they sat back well fed, they were offered an Irish coffee. To a girl whose only experience of whisky was when her mother put a spoonful out of bottle kept 'for medicinal purposes' in hot orange juice as a cure for a bad cold, the daring idea of a tot of whisky in a cup of strong black coffee topped off with a thick layer of cream was pure bliss. And best of all, this gorgeous meal had not cost them as much as they had expected. This was another plus in Berni's favour, the prices were not only very reasonable – by 1969 the main meal had risen to 8/6d (42½p) – they were the same everywhere.

Chinese restaurants had long been part of the larger towns and seaside resorts, offering the lure of something exotic, later added to by Indian restaurants, which early on provided a take-away service as well. This gave the choice of a relaxed evening seated amidst the evocative décor of highly-embossed dark wallpaper or strange scenes, heavily painted in reds and gold on the walls. The lighting was usually very subdued and while one's nose was filled with the pervasive smell of curry, the strange sounds of Indian music played gently on the ear. Eating out for the first time in either type of establishment was something of an adventure – and to some seemed very daring. Alternatively, a group of friends might opt for a take-away curry at the home of one of them. This was a much more relaxed way to enjoy the food and worked out cheaper too! Fifty years on it seems strange to think that until the Chinese and Indian restaurants started 'a carry-out service' the only take-away cooked food available was that from the fish and chip shop.

Those who could afford to eat out occasionally at restaurants were constantly being educated about food that was new to them. Italian establishments showed them there was more to pasta than spaghetti and macaroni and were surprising them with very different types of bread, as well as introducing customers to the use of both olives and olive oil. Similarly, Greek, French and Spanish restaurants showed off their cuisine to a nation with a reputation stolidly set on a diet of meat and two veg, one of which had to be potatoes in some form. Women eating out became interested in this tempting of their taste buds and set about trying to recreate at home dishes they had enjoyed out. From this it was just one step nearer to inviting friends to share what one had cooked and so began the trend for supper parties.

'Our social life' wrote P.T., 'at that time was mostly having friends round or visiting them on a Saturday night taking the children with us, first in carrycots and later in sleeping bags so they could sleep and be transported home in a half-asleep state. Learning to cook new things was fun and a lot of different foreign recipes were tried out to get away from the boring meat and two veg British diet of the post-war years.' And baby came too, became a common practice in the 1960s. They may have had to share the spare bedroom with the guests' coats but there was always someone ready to report a crying infant and mother was on hand to feed it if necessary.

While entertaining friends was part of Sixties women's leisure, they also found time for many other activities. Although television was mentioned, particularly by those with young children, it had not yet become as much a part of their lives as it is today. By the Sixties there were three channels operating, BBC One and Two and ITV, which had introduced us to goods we had never thought of through advertisements. The standard of many of these was such that they were almost mini sagas in themselves. However, not only were 1960s viewers restricted to three channels, they were also limited to the number of hours broadcast daily.

I was twenty-two when we married in 1966. We lived in Harlow and after a very lonely start, we plucked up the courage to join the Harlow 18 Plus club. This met once a week in a room behind a pub and we had a programme of speakers, entertainers etc. The best part was that the members were a complete cross-section of society so we met a lot of non-academic people, which was a nice change. Folk music and Traditional jazz were very popular at the time and we spent a lot of time in smoke-filled rooms at jazz and folk clubs. We also did American square dancing and loved to watch the Morris dancers. There was also a very active social club where we worked. The labs were built on a country estate with a big country house and grounds. We played croquet and did archery at lunch times. We would also have holiday-slide evenings, which I loved and also a stamp club, which was the ultimate in nerd-dom, but which I also loved. There were also quite a few affairs going on between members of staff – the whole nature of this rather isolated complex of laboratories lent itself to this kind of behaviour.

J.T.'s mention of holiday-slide evenings draws attention to the tremendous development in the camera industry, which took place in the 1960s. Most families had owned, or at least had access to, the well-known pre-war Box Brownie camera, which was slowly replaced by more superior models still using reels of black-and-white film. Colour film was in vogue by the 1960s but alas, many of us who have photographs dating from then have found that the colour has faded or taken on an orange tint. Since for a time black and white film became difficult to buy, many were forced to use colour instead. As cameras became more sophisticated, keen photographers opted to have their films developed not as printed pictures to be displayed in an album but as slides, which could be shown through a projector on to a screen. This meant that one could plan a whole programme of entertainment for a group of family or friends. Alongside this were those who opted for the 8mm cine camera. For a family this was a wonderful innovation: never mind the snapshot of baby digging his first sandcastle, proud parents could now capture all those precious moments on a moving film. One contributor when asked to search for photographs that might illustrate her account was somewhat taken aback when going through her late parents' photographs, she discovered there were absolutely none of her during the 1960s except the formal wedding ones. She wondered for a moment what she could have done to cause this dearth and then she remembered that her father had been taken up with a cine camera at that time.

Sixties women were prepared to make their own amusement to fill their leisure hours. Those with an interest in the theatre would join with other like-minded men and women at a local amateur dramatic society often presenting two or three productions a year for the entertainment of the public – and themselves. Such ventures not only gave budding actors a chance to display their talent but also needed the expertise of electricians, scenery makers, painters and gifted women who could take old material and turn it into costumes. Many who were roped into joining a group by a friend or husband or wife discovered they had latent talents. A play-reading group was the answer for those who did not wish to perform in public. Several contributors met their partners this way, as others did by joining music groups. If one had a good voice then a choir was the answer, via a choral or operatic society. The latter might include a group devoted to Gilbert and Sullivan operettas. Music, of course, has many genres and as we know the Sixties was very much the era of popular music. Aside from the well-known like The Beatles, The Rolling Stones, The Beach Boys, Cliff Richard, et al, most towns, even very small ones, had their own groups of guitar, bass and drum playing young men either copying the 'stars' or writing their own music, who appealed mainly to the younger women. So we have people like T., H. and others who followed their own local groups on a Saturday night as they performed in coffee bars and pubs. F., for example, wrote: 'The place to go was Bluesville in the summer and the Baths Hall in the winter. [The swimming pool was covered over to make a dance floor.] There would be a lot of well-known singers and bands appearing, including Rod "the Mod" Stewart. A local band, Nick and the Nomads, was very popular with the Mods and we tried to attend all their gigs'. How amused their grandchildren would be to know that 'granny' was one of the original groupies.

Jazz clubs, which had built up keen devotees in the Fifties, found a whole new audience among the young twenty-somethings in the Sixties. Influenced, as so much else was from the United States, the talent of home-grown musicians like Kenny Baker, Johnny Dankworth and Acker Bilk was also much appreciated. At a time when the guitar, bass and drums were so much in evidence, many music lovers welcomed the clarity of sound that these artistes could produce from saxophones and clarinets. Half a century later the haunting sound of Acker Bilk's rendition of 'Moon River' can send shivers down the spine – provided one can ignore its use in a modern advertisement.

Again, influenced by the American Country and Western music, folk music had a devoted, if smaller, following in this country. Both forms reintroduced a more formalised style of dancing than was generally popular at the time. But square dancing and traditional folk dances while requiring concentration to perform brought the addition of benefit to health as well as comradeship. It would be an unintended pun to say that circle dancing, for example, widened one's circle of friends! Dancing at that time was very much a hotchpotch. The Victor Sylvester studios and the lesser-known dancing schools were still teaching strict ballroom dances. Schoolgirls still learnt the basic waltz and quickstep and possibly the Cha cha cha to be able to hold their own at the Saturday night hop, though they were much happier just jiving or 'bopping'. Their mothers and older sisters mastered the Twist, which was one of many strange dances to sweep not only this country but everywhere in the world where groups of expatriates were to be found. The more formal charity balls and firms' dinner dances usually had a live band, which played a mixture of ballroom and more up-to-date dances.

It would appear that 1960s women went to the theatre more often than their 21st-century counterparts. This could be explained by the very wide range of dramatic works offered by present day television companies, though it is certain that current economics also play their part. In the Sixties, for those living in or within easy reach of London, it was possible to obtain really cheap seats to witness first-class performances, as J.K. recorded:

Often queued at the Royal Opera House (once all night after the end of term ball at college) to get a queue ticket which gave you time to return and purchase tickets for the ballet on the first day of booking. That way you could get the best of the cheap tickets up in the 'gods' for the new season's productions. Those were the days of Fonteyn and Nureyev, Antoinette Sibley, Anthony Dowell, Lynn Seymour, Michael Coleman and Wayne Sleep. Favourite ballet probably Prokofiev's *Romeo and Juliet* ... Also became an associate member of the Royal Shakespeare Company which gave you priority booking, cheap tickets for press reviews etc as the RSC were based at The Aldwych in those days, a stone's throw from King's College. Saw just about all their productions in the mid to late 1960s. Peter Brooke's *Midsummer Night's Dream*, Peter Hall's productions with brilliant actors such as Helen Mirren, Glenda Jackson, Ian Holm, David Warner, Frances de la Tour, Vivienne Marchant in Pinter's *The Homecoming*. One of the plays, *US*, was about Vietnam.

Most of those who studied in London also describe queuing for cheap seats; these were not necessarily those in the 'gods' – sometimes they were lucky enough to get 'returns', tickets that had been bought in advance and returned to the box office for resale because the original buyer was unable to attend that evening. Our drama student wrote: 'I did see a lot of live theatre as a student, for we would get free tickets when someone special was performing in London, for example the Russian State Theatre playing *The Cherry Orchard* and Antonioni, the Spanish Flamenco dancer.' Hospitals also were in regular receipt of free tickets, not just in London but wherever there was a theatre. When the Royal Ballet Company's tour included the north-west of England, student nurse S.T. went to see performances two weeks running, an opportunity that would have rarely come her way otherwise. Often the receipt of free tickets opened a young woman's eyes to a genre of music or a branch of the theatre which was entirely new to her. Classical music may have been something she had never considered but a trip to a concert with a group of friends could awaken responses she would never have thought possible. One woman admitted she had not wanted to go and sit for a couple of hours at the Festival Hall on a Sunday evening but she was reduced to tears when she heard a programme of Chopin for the first time and thereafter was converted to adding classical music to her listening. Not everyone responded in this way however, one woman had a newly acquired boyfriend who took her to Covent Garden Opera House and in the expensive seats at that. What he did not tell her was that the Wagner opera they would see/hear was very long and to her utter embarrassment, she fell asleep, though fortunately not for long and he accepted her explanation that it was the warmth of the theatre that had induced her behaviour rather than her utter boredom.

Although many living outside London would save up for a trip to the capital, which would include a visit to a West End theatre, those living in the provinces were not denied theatrical performances for most of the large towns still had a viable repertory theatre. A different play would be performed every two or three weeks by the members of the company. It was there that most of the actors who went on to make their names in films and television honed the skills they had learned in drama school and worked to achieve the Equity card which recognised that they were truly members of the acting profession. Many of those living in different parts of the country developed not only a love of the theatre – often at fraction of the cost of a seat in the West End – but also widened their knowledge of drama as the 'Rep' produced everything from Ibsen, Chekov and Shakespeare, to Noel Coward, Pinter and Wesker, among others. Those who lived within reach of Stratford-upon-Avon were able to enjoy Shakespeare in the beautiful theatre there. Some contributors recall that as sixth-formers studying English A level, they were taken by their teacher at the end of the summer term of 1961 for a week's study based on Stratford. They had their own bus to take them around by day to explore the area and all the Shakespeare associations and on three evenings they attended performances. For some it was the first time they had stayed in an hotel, albeit a very small one. On the way home on the Friday, they stopped to explore Bath with all its associations with Jane Austen, also part of their exam syllabus.

The cinema was still a very popular way to spend an evening out and the 1960s produced some outstanding and thought-provoking films. *Dr Zhivago* is the one mentioned most by contributors followed by *Billy Liar*, *The Entertainer* and *Lawrence of Arabia*. Obviously this is not the place to list all the other favourite or memorable films that were mentioned but the Internet will provide lists of films that were either made or were being shown during the decade. Some will be familiar from their constant showing on television. Most surprising is the wide choice to suit all tastes; comedy in the likes of the 'Carry On' series, the 'Doctor' films, and those of Norman Wisdom; romances; horror; thrillers, and dramas written by the best writers of the day, many of them dealing with social and political concerns of the time. The film *Tom Jones*, adapted from Fielding's novel of the same name, was mentioned by the group of Dorset school friends who were studying in London. The reason they went en masse to the Odeon in Leicester Square to see it was because they had all appeared in it, somewhere. Filmed on location in their part of Dorset, they were allowed time off school after their exams to act as stand-ins, double for the leading lady in riding scenes, or act as members of the crowd. We can only hope that they did not disturb too many of the audience near them by loud whispers as they recognised their fellows.

Nightclubs had long been part of the social scene for those who could afford them. They were mainly situated in London and were the playgrounds of the rich and famous about whom we read or saw photographed in magazines and the Sunday papers, but they certainly were not for 'the likes of us'. So M.J. was somewhat taken aback when the wife of one of her husband's colleagues invited them to join a party that was going to a nightclub in Colchester. What should she wear? Full-length evening dress seemed to be worn by celebrities or would a cocktail dress be more appropriate? As the woman who had issued the invitation had never been to this establishment before, they chose the safer option of the shorter dress. Keyed up with excitement they approached the premises, which turned out to have a narrow frontage in a side street and looked as if, in a previous existence, it had been a small shop. Once inside they found themselves in a largish room, set with tables around a miniscule dance floor. Their party was the only one there and it soon became obvious that this was little more than a Greek restaurant. 'What can you expect at eight o'clock in the evening?' someone asked. Those who knew about these things commented that of course in London, nightclubs were just that, they functioned late at night till the early hours of the morning. So, they had their meal and when the music was switched on, they took advantage of the dancing area, which just about accommodated four couples. It was not at all what M.J. had anticipated but she was later able to shock her mother-in-law by announcing that they had been to a nightclub.

Active participation in a sport was important to many women, particularly if they had enjoyed it at school. Those studying at universities and colleges were encouraged to do so, Wednesday afternoons were often free of lectures so that they could practise hockey or netball in preparation for matches on Saturday. Girls who did not go on to further education had the choice of joining a local club, or if they worked for large firms, they were often provided with excellent sports facilities for both winter and summer sports as well as indoor ones like badminton and squash. Keen swimmers could join the club at their local swimming baths. There were also athletic clubs for those whose interests lay in that direction. One contributor told of joining an archery class run by the Local Education Authority as an evening class. Not having been very good at sports at school she thought this might suit her, telling herself that walking back and forth to retrieve her arrows was good healthy exercise. She found she not only enjoyed it but was actually hitting the target more than missing it, until the day came when she realised that being in the later stages of pregnancy, she could no longer hold her bow properly!

Many couples enjoyed walking. There were those who took pleasure in strolling through parks and the countryside on a fine day over the weekend; the activity gave them time to talk after a busy week at work, as well as giving them some much needed fresh air and exercise but best of all, it did not cost them anything. What better way too, to explore an area in which they were now living; for example the deserted streets of the City of London when all the businesses were closed had much to reveal to the historically minded. For the more serious walkers there were Rambling Clubs all over the country, which met weekly and undertook to follow an interesting route covering at the least five miles, before ending up at a country pub for a drink and a bag of crisps. In those far off days, public houses did not provide meals. Several of the contributors came from Cumbria and for them there was the opportunity of fell walking – or running for the very keen – and even the odd spot of climbing. All these activities could be undertaken with a boyfriend, husband or a group of fellow enthusiasts. Although several mentioned cycling as a leisure activity, none reported that they had taken up fishing!

All the women who contributed mentioned listening to music, which of course fits in so well with the stereotypical view of the 1960s. The radio – or wireless as the older generation still called it – provided much of it. The little transistor radios which came in during the period offered the younger population the chance to carry music with them wherever they went. Several women told of curling up in bed on Sunday evening to listen to Radio Luxemburg, then the only commercial radio station. There one could hear the top twenty tunes of the week. Later during the decade came the pirate radio stations, ships anchored in the North Sea just outside British territorial waters, which played continuous popular music and introduced listeners to the exciting world of the DJ or disc jockey like Tony Blackburn and others. Television also catered for music fans with programmes such as *Top of the Pops* and *Juke Box Jury*, avidly watched mostly by the younger generation. A student in Exeter in 1969, V. tells something of her life there. 'We had the joys of the weekly wash at the local launderette. We chose one with a colour TV and did the wash on Thursday night to watch *Top of the Pops* ... I have just realised that none of the digs we occupied had TVs for us to watch. We had our radios.' And if they could not get enough news of what was going on in the world of pop, then there were magazines that catered just for them. Who nowadays remembers *The Boyfriend* magazine? Its hardback annual for 1961 was expensive at 10/6d but no doubt was a much-requested Christmas present for thousands of teenage girls. It was full of coloured plates of the leading singing idols, with Cliff Richard hailed as 'star of the year'. Many of those featured retained their popularity while others like Mark Wynter and Anthony Newley went on to become film stars. Others, as is the way of show business, just disappeared from the public's consciousness. The style of the magazine itself was very American in tone. Strip cartoons for easy reading were interspersed with romantic short stories. These were similar in theme to those in British magazines of the previous decade and the first years of the 1960s, namely that of the shy, retiring, undiscovered beauty, who finally attained stardom – and got her man! Strangest of all, for what was essentially a pop music-oriented magazine, there were also sections on cookery – the way to a man's heart, perhaps? – as well as patterns for knitting for leisure and pleasure. The real musical magazine that was read by both sexes was *The New Musical Express*, known amongst its followers simply as the *NME*.

For the post-teenager, and particular the married woman, it would be safe to assume that practically every one of them, at one time or another, filled part of their leisure time reading magazines specifically aimed at them. Whether they actually bought them regularly is not clear. Certainly the weekly magazines, *Woman*, *Woman's Own* and *Woman's Weekly* had a huge circulation. Those issued monthly, *Everywoman*, *Homes and Gardens*, *Good Housekeeping*, *Harpers Bazaar*, *Country Life* and *The Tatler*, appealed to the older and more affluent women although when back copies of them appeared on the table in the dentist's or doctor's waiting room, then who could resist a browse through to discover how the other half lived? Then there were the specialist craft magazines like *Stitchcraft* and *Pins and Needles* and in a niche all of its own, *The Lady*, with its mixture of sensible articles and discreet advertisements for domestic posts both wanted and vacant, breathed an air of gentility that was already in danger of disappearing.

The content of these magazines provided their readers with much more than a quick read to fill in a few minutes of leisure time. Attractively produced in various-sized formats, often using colour for the covers and for some illustrations and at an affordable price, the range of subjects between the covers, although following a standard pattern in most cases, was indeed wide enough to suit all tastes. For those who had not the time to read a whole book, there were usually two or three short stories. These were always well written by professional writers, many of whom acquired a following of readers for their full-length novels. Often the short story was both human and humorous, poking gentle fun at aspects of family life. Occasionally a serious note was introduced with a crime threatening to destroy a peaceful neighbourhood, similar perhaps to the more restrained cases in *Midsomer Murders*. For those who wanted something longer and more absorbing there were serialised novels. These tended to follow a similar pattern; a young heroine in a setting out of the norm, whether it be in a foreign country (the Australian Outback, New Zealand or Africa were all popular locations) or a remote location in the British Isles. Add in a mysterious strong male character who either takes no notice of her or does his best to disparage her; throw in a beautiful, slim, blonde female out to entrap the tall dark man and you have the basis for the many variations on the theme that has entranced readers since Charlotte Brontë penned *Jane Eyre*.

Magazines inspired great loyalty amongst readers who were quite likely to quote 'my magazine' as a fount of knowledge, which indeed it was on many subjects. Those that appeared monthly were larger in size and pages so could offer their readers long, illustrated articles taking them, for example, on a visit to the Queen Mother's Scottish home, the Castle of Mey; or to Lamb House at Rye, once the home of the American writer Henry James, but at the time of writing in 1969, home to the writer Rumer Godden. It seems our thirst for celebrity gossip has a long history, particularly when it concerns royalty Another monthly magazine dating from 1964 included an article which considered which foreign princess might be the future bride of Prince Charles. He was sixteen at the time!

Perhaps, without readers realising it, their favourite magazine provided them with a mother substitute, especially those who were living miles away from their own mothers. Such was the tone of the magazine that it offered sensible advice on a multitude of subjects from bringing up children, cooking, sewing and knitting, where to find goods, seek help with financial matters, discuss medical and matrimonial problems through to where to go for a holiday. The list was endless.

Most of the women who helped with this study of the 1960s listed reading as a favourite leisure activity. Most made great use of their local libraries as well as building up collections of their own of favourite authors. The publishers Penguin and Dent were both producing books that were affordable, the former issuing paperback editions of current novels and plays as well as other genres, while Dent's Everyman Library hardback editions meant that a reader could build up her own library of the classics. D.R., who lived in Cumbria, was delighted when she discovered Hugh Walpole's historical novels, 'The Herries Chronicles' set in the Lake District. M.T., on the other hand, went through a phase of reading books by women writers, for example, Edna O'Brien, Winifred Holtby and Germaine Greer ('I hated her excessive feminism') but was then introduced by her brother to John le Carré's books which she greatly enjoyed. Perhaps the reading habits of women in the 1960s can best be summed up by T.: 'I always had my nose in a book. I can't actually remember what sort of thing I read.' T. also related that whilst still at school she had attempted to borrow *East of Eden* from the school library. She was told she would need a parental note to do so. Surely there was no better incitement to read the book!

For most people there was a prolonged period of leisure for two weeks in the year when they took their annual holiday from work. Not everyone could afford to go away from home for that length of time and some just could not afford to go away at all. For these, what is nowadays given the rather pretentious title of a 'staycation' was, in the 1960s known simply as a 'holiday at home'. This usually entailed days out, taking advantage of cheap fares on the bus or train, to the nearest seaside resort or into the countryside, anywhere the family, and it usually was a family, did not have to spend too much money. J. recalled: 'We didn't have much money but we had a lot of fun with our children, days out on picnics at the river or at the beach and weekends with my parents. I can remember someone lending us a caravan in Felixstowe. A whole week away on just a week's pay! We were in the sea every day, but we didn't go anywhere near the amusements as we had no money to spend! But we had a great time.'

For families who could afford it, then a week at Butlins or a similar holiday camp was the ideal answer. The accommodation was basic by modern standards, the food plentiful but hardly cordon bleu, but the entertainment for all age groups was unsurpassable. There were activities for them all, throughout the day and in the evenings. When the children were tucked up in bed, with staff patrols keeping an ear out for any crying, then the parents could relax and enjoy a professional-standard variety show, followed by dancing to a live band. For the gregarious this type of holiday was hard to beat. Some families went year after year and many a young woman had her first taste of showbusiness when she entered the camp's talent contest. Each week's winner could win a free holiday for her family. This was also the great era of the bathing beauty contest and each year one, of the many young women who were successful winners of the week on their holiday, went on to be crowned the Holiday Princess of the Year in the final contest of the season. For some this started them on the road to national and even international beauty contests. Unfortunately, efforts to find a 1960s winner of such a contest willing to talk about her life on the beauty queen circuit proved fruitless; it would have been interesting to hear of the reality behind the glitz and glamour.

Package holidays abroad and the growth of air travel in the late 1950s had opened up new holiday destinations for the woman seeking something different. Travel companies offered an all-inclusive travel, food and accommodation package (hence the name) at an affordable price. Whether it were a ferry crossing with a long coach drive to the Costa Brava or a charter flight to Italy, it was still very much a group activity. For young women venturing abroad for the first time with a girl friend, this could be reassuring. One might not be immediately drawn to all one's fellow travellers but at least they spoke English and might be called upon if one ran into a spot of bother. For example, if, during an evening out, some of the local males were becoming over-attentive, it was good to know that if one saw the elderly couple, who always sat at the next table in your hotel, having a quiet drink, you could join them and escape the unwanted attention.

Fortunately no such problem faced S.T.:

I took my first trip by air in 1961. My friend and I went to Jersey. We were so excited; we bought travel insurance at the airport and forgot to post it before we travelled! The highlight of our holiday was that we met Mat Monroe [the singer] and Bernie Winters [half of the duo Mike and Bernie Winters, popular TV comedians] in a jewellery shop. They gave us their autographs.

A few years later R was, like many other students, hitchhiking, accepting lifts in cars and lorries without giving it a second thought. 'I hitch-hiked in France – having philosophical discussions with lorry drivers! Camping and sightseeing – all on a shoestring. I had a little au pair job with a French family to avoid having to return to the UK when the money ran out.'

Other students took advantage of the cheap holidays offered by the National Union of Students (NUS) to places like Norway, Austria and Italy. Others, not necessarily students, went on working holidays to various parts of Africa and India while others stayed in this country and undertook paid holidays in the countryside, fruit and pea picking; helping on newly set-up organic farms or in setting up the early communes that intended to practise ecological living. Worthy and worthwhile as all of these were, all holidays in the 1960s were governed by economy. One of the advantages of a package was that once it had been paid for, the holidaymaker knew that she would only need to spend out on extras, such as the occasional drink or ice cream. Camping sounded a cheap way of doing things but if it were on the Continent then site fees and all food would have to be paid for out of one's allowance. Today, one gives little thought to such matters, a credit card can be used in any part of the world but in 1960s Britain, the government would not permit you to take more than a small amount of money out of the country. The amount you paid for foreign currency or travellers' cheques was stamped in your passport. At one stage this was as little as £15 per person but by 1969 when D. and her husband set off to Canada, the personal allowance was raised to £50. They were able to spend almost five weeks seeing as much of the huge country as they could – but only because they relied on the great generosity of D.'s Canadian cousins who provided them with hospitality.

In the early Sixties Majorca was a popular destination for honeymooners. As most couples married on Saturday, some of the charter airlines ran special flights for newlyweds on Sundays. The last Saturday before 5 April was always a busy day for weddings, as the bridegroom, now classed as a married man, could reclaim the difference in tax that he had paid as a single man in the previous twelve months. Consequently flights on the Sunday following were heavily booked and always featured in the TV and cinema newsreels at the time. The Channel Islands and the Lake District were the next most favoured places mentioned by correspondents both for holidays and honeymoons. Each married contributor emphasised that holidays abroad ceased once they were saving for a house and had children. The advent of a family meant that the couple were likely to return to the more conventional British seaside holiday in a caravan or boarding house. Unlike on the Continent, children were not made welcome in many hotels and certainly not in public houses. In 1968 one woman and her husband were asked to leave a deserted country pub at lunchtime when it was discovered they had a tiny sleeping baby with them. The licensee suggested they leave the baby in the car in the car park. As for hotels those which did accept children insisted they had their evening meal before the main dinner was served. While parents appreciated that having small children in the dining room might disturb other guests, this often meant that the parents alternated in having their meal, with the other staying with the child. No wonder that as soon as they were able to afford it, families took to the Continent for their holidays, but that came later.

Chapter Ten

Financial Pressures

The children and grandchildren of the 1960s women constantly insist that life in the twenty-first century is very hard for them and that 'it wasn't like that in your day!' They bemoan that they are unable to obtain mortgages; that prices are so high, comparing Grandma's proud boast that she could fill up her car with four gallons of petrol for £1 whereas now they are looking at more than twenty times that amount. It is useless for Grandma to remonstrate that money comparisons are useless, pointing out that they probably earn almost as much in a month as she did in a year. Times may have changed in so many ways but a phrase that was repeated over and over in these recollections, particularly by married women, was 'money was tight'.

Whatever the young may believe, very few newly-married couples started their life together in a brand-new house 'which cost hardly anything compared to today', fully furnished and equipped with all the labour-saving devices. As we have discovered elsewhere, 'home' for the majority consisted of a couple of rooms rented in someone else's house, sharing their kitchen and bathroom. Sometimes, if the parental home of one of them was big enough, then they might occupy two of the rooms there. The advantage of this was that the rent was likely to be low, perhaps a token payment towards electricity bills. The disadvantage was that if it was the girl's parents' house, her mother was likely to treat her as if she was still single and tell her what she should be doing, while the husband's mother was likely to be critical of her efforts. Either way, discord was likely to arise somewhere to upset the new relationship.

Luckier were the couples who, having secured a job in one of the new towns, were allocated a well-designed flat in one of the blocks of flats that were helping to create the new community. For those earning an above-average salary, the rents were considered reasonable. In London and elsewhere, the local councils were charged with a duty to provide decent housing and blocks of flats seemed to be the answer. However, while the flats were being built, tenants were allocated on a basis of need. This covered those families who for one reason or another needed to be re-housed but also those members of the public who were considered to be essential to the local area, such as teachers, nurses, firemen and police. Apart from the tower blocks built in large towns most of the council-built flats of the period tended to be three- or four-storeyed, with a balcony outside either the kitchen or living room, accessed through a half-glazed door, where one dried the washing or tried to have the semblance of a garden with a few plant pots. One woman, who lived in such a block for the time when her husband was seconded to the area on a short-term contract, recounted how, sitting alone one summer evening around nine o'clock, her attention was taken from her book by movement outside the window. Imagine her amazement when, very slowly, a wardrobe passed downwards, followed minutes later from the floor above (she was on the third), by a sofa and then a mattress, rapidly followed by the bed frame. A shower of bedding, cushions and clothing sailed after, at which point curiosity got the better of her and she looked down at the road below where a lorry was being loaded with all the items. It took time for her to realise that she was watching something she had only ever read about in old novels, 'a moonlight flit'!

It probably took most couples two years to save the deposit needed to apply for a mortgage. Getting a mortgage was as big a problem in the 1960s as it has been throughout the last fifty years. It was a sign of the old fashioned, slightly misogynistic attitude of the commercial and legal world that, except in very special circumstances, mortgages could be given only to men. It was understood that a man should seek to borrow over a term of twenty or twenty-five years not less than the equivalent of two and a half times his salary. Often this meant that a couple who had fallen in love with a particular house were unable to buy it because the man's salary fell short. By the 1960s, women were earning high wages and in some cases they earned more than their husbands. Could they not, many argued, have their wages taken into account? Shock, horror! Certainly not, was the reply, you are a woman and you will have children and be unable to work, therefore your wages cannot possibly be considered. One woman did actually manage to circumvent the system – at a cost. A schoolteacher living in Kent, she had, prior to her marriage, had a mortgage secured by an insurance policy backed by her Union on a house she shared with her mother. On her marriage the house was sold to provide funds for a house for her mother. Later when her husband was refused a mortgage, she decided to investigate the possibility of using her salary too. At the time the mortgage rate generally was around

5–6 per cent but she heard that the local council had funds it was lending at 8 per cent. So she applied to the Council, was subjected to a grilling interview and was granted a joint mortgage with her husband on condition that in the event of her having a child, she would return to work at the earliest possible moment having arranged reliable childcare.

Fortunately her husband was not one of that generation of younger men who, in the very early days of the 1960s believed, as their fathers had done, that once they married it was their duty to support their wife who in turn would see it as her duty to look after him, the home and, in due time, the children. The idea that his wife should go out to work was anathema to many who felt that to do so would reflect on his inability to provide. This attitude seems to have been more prevalent amongst the men who had gone from school into work, living at home until marriage, all the time remaining in the same location. To the outsider it looks as if they merely exchanged mother for wife – expecting that wife would be able to do all that mother had done, which in most cases meant taking care of all his needs. These were the 1950s mothers who had proper hot lunches, 'complete with apple pie and custard' (as one contributor described it) promptly on the table when son and father came home each day. That particular mother continued to bake a chocolate cake each week for her son long after his marriage.

Things were slightly better where men who had cut the apron strings were concerned. Those who had experience of living perhaps in a hall of residence if they were in higher education were still looked after in as far as their meals were provided but they had to learn to eat what was presented to them and they were expected to keep their rooms tidy. Others who moved away to work went into lodgings where they discovered that landladies were not so amenable as mother had been. Then there were those in big towns and cities who opted for life in a bedsitter which meant being responsible for looking after themselves entirely, learning the hard way how to cook either in a kitchen shared with the other lodgers or on a gas ring in their room. The next step was to share a flat with another man, although as a popular television comedy of the time depicted, a man and two girls was a possibility. That was a young man's dream, not least because he hoped the girls could cook!

Women and girls who were well qualified for the job they were doing were often earning good wages; in the teaching profession for example, equal pay had been achieved in the late Fifties. Although young nurses were still notoriously badly paid and, unlike those who worked in factories, did not receive extra for overtime or time and a half for weekends and bank holidays, they knew their pay would increase with promotion. With the expanding industrial scene and new technology, as well as the growth in tourism in all its aspects, the jobs' market for women was increasing all the time, as T. commented, 'I got a job straight away. Looking back, it seemed that getting a job was easy'. Another woman said that when she wanted to go away for a long summer holiday, she simply gave up her job, knowing full well that she would be able to walk into another on her return. Thus many women were reluctant to give up work on marriage. Used to buying clothes and make up when they wanted; having holidays abroad and pursuing hobbies; not having to think if they could afford to go out for a meal or visit the theatre or cinema, all these things influenced a woman's decision as to whether she should be a stay-at-home wife initially.

'Early married life was not easy', wrote M.O. 'Money was short. I carried on working for two years. We had very little in the way of furniture and it was quite difficult to save whilst paying the mortgage. Most of my birthday presents were items for the home; it was not very exciting to receive a frying pan or ironing board for a Christmas present'. M.O. had to stop work when her daughter was born at the end of 1963.

> The plan was to be a stay-at-home Mum but money was still tight and I thought about returning to work but this was difficult once you had children. I was able to find work to do at home. I did the accounts for my Dad's shop, preparing the takings ready to go to the bank, paying the bills and so on. For this I received thirty shillings a week – not much, but it helped. Later I found another job that I could do at home; I painted cake decorations, thousands upon thousands of little robins to go on chocolate logs. These had to be packed into bags ready for delivery to bakeries. I also painted Father Christmas and Snowman plaques to go on top of cakes. These took longer to do and although the rate of pay was higher I could not do enough to satisfy the supplier. For this I was paid about twenty-five shillings a week. My husband was working very long hours so I was able to do this work when the children were in bed. Sometimes I worked into the small hours.

Many women undertook home work of various types. In most cases it amounted to 'sweated labour' for very poor financial returns and as M.O. indicated, the home-worker was penalised if she failed to fulfil the required quota on time. Sewing a covered button onto the centre of a cushion may sound easy but when faced with a hundred at a time it was tedious to say the least. Addressing envelopes or folding leaflets to go into envelopes were among the more mind-numbing but more straightforward jobs. One woman had an addressograph machine, 'a huge hulking thing in my kitchen for several years to earn money as we were struggling. I basically tapped out addresses onto metal plates, I suppose for firms to use.' At least both the previous woman and M.O. had the shelter of their homes. In contrast J., who lived in the country, had to rely on field work to supplement her family's income. Taking her two small children with her she picked currants and apples and endured the backbreaking lifting of potatoes. But she was young; she had had her first child at eighteen and because this was seasonal work she also had a variety of evening jobs. Like ships that pass in the night, she went to work when her husband came home to be with the children. Once they were at school, however, she was able to find a day job.

Finding work that would fit in not only with the school day but also the school holidays was a problem that for a number was solved by becoming 'a dinner lady'. D.T.'s husband did not like the thought of her going out to work so she initially made her contribution to the family pot by acting as an agent for a catalogue company. This not only brought in funds it also helped her to get to know the many families who moved into the new council estate just after she did. Buying from one of the many catalogue companies of the period was a boon for many who were on restricted incomes. The small weekly payments without any added interest meant that there was no longer any need to actually save up before one bought. And, as D.T. found, the two shillings in the pound commission the agents received was most welcome; so many women who had never before been involved with handling money or keeping records became agents and the more successful they were, the more they earned. In D.T.'s case the time came when even this income was not sufficient to meet the extra demands on the family's outgoings, and with both children at school, her husband finally agreed to her applying for the job which would fit in with both the school day and the school holidays, which happened to be at the local school helping to prepare and serve the hot dinners that were provided for the children. In those days many parents, especially if they lived some distance from the school, took advantage of their child having a reasonably-priced hot meal midday. With changing work-patterns generally, many men now had their meal provided by a work's canteen. This meant the housewife could concentrate on providing a high tea for her family. This of course, depended on individual families: there were some men who stolidly refused to give up their home-cooked hot dinner being on the table at the dot of one o'clock, regardless of whether or not the children came home, while many secondary-school children were expected to cycle two or three miles home to eat a meal and then cycle back for the afternoon session.

F., who lived in a village which had a very sparse bus service, found that suitable work opportunities within cycling distance were almost non-existent. She too became a dinner lady, regarding herself as fortunate, as such jobs had become almost like gold dust. News of a possible vacancy was passed on by word of mouth long before the advertisement for it appeared in the local newspaper. A highly-qualified secretary, yet, when the dinner serving job ended, F. was not too proud to take on cleaning at a boarding school within cycling distance. This she did in the evenings when her husband was home from work and could look after their daughters. Having proved herself to be efficient and reliable, she was later asked to become an evening supervisor of the boarders.

Women with secretarial skills who lived in urban areas were often able to get casual work at home from big companies or to type up dissertations for university students; some tried their hand at writing short stories for magazines but this was unlikely to produce a regular income. Those who possessed a sewing machine could in time build up a small business making women's and children's clothes, while the careful knitter could not only sell her garments locally, there was a demand from large department stores, especially in London, which regularly employed outworkers for hand knitted garments. That in turn provided another job for the stay-at-home mother, as the distributor of wool to the knitters and collector and inspector of the finished garments to be sent off to the store concerned. Other women could make a few extra shillings a week by baking; those who were really skilled were in demand to bake wedding and birthday cakes. Others who had perfected the art of intricate icing for cakes could command a good fee, though far less than the shop would charge. The products of their homemaking skills that women developed, such as making bread, jams, marmalade, lemon curd, chutney and preserving fruit could all find buyers amongst friends and neighbours but a steady income was there for the Women's Institute members who sold their wares at the weekly W.I. market. Similarly, the woman who loved her garden could sell her surplus fruit and vegetables. There was no end to the possibilities open to those who needed either to earn or simply keep their minds occupied.

A major women's magazine from the mid-Sixties recognised the need for women to supplement either the family income or to give themselves some pin money by running an article with some suggestions both for the women who were able to do casual work during school hours as well as those who were still tied to the home. A 'guinea-pig' tried out the various suggestions and reported on her personal reactions while also giving useful contact addresses for further information. Amongst the suggestions were some that are still available, for example the selling of cosmetic products. This, we were told, was a good way to make money and meet new people too, especially if the sales lady could persuade a customer to hostess a party in her home. This type of party selling was probably most successful with the advent of Tupperware; not everyone wants a new lipstick and eye shadow but most women wanted storage boxes and previously unthought-of gadgets for the home.

For the woman who did not mind being the centre of attention, had a pleasant manner and liked people, then there was the opportunity to be an in-store demonstrator. This job had the advantage that the demonstrator was kept on her toes, as she never knew quite what it was she would be attempting to sell to the public. It might be the latest kitchen gadget – the wonder knife or the plastic vegetable grater – to a new variety of packet mix for cakes or different ways to serve tinned asparagus. However, the drawback to demonstrating was that it was not regular, a woman had to be available on an 'as and when' basis. However, at least the woman was working inside an establishment.

It was a different story for those who were engaged as market researchers. Often this work was available only to those who lived in towns and they had to be prepared to stand in the street with their clipboards and accost passers-by for their opinions on whatever was the chosen topic. On the whole people in the 1960s were fairly polite and if they had not time to stop they would offer an apology and walk away but the researcher had to be prepared for rebuffs. They also had to possess an ability to judge a passer-by's age group and be discreet in their approach to someone they thought might fit into the age bracket that the particular survey they were conducting required. Better to tell a lady that she was too young to be questioned even if one was pretty sure she was not. So, self-confidence and tact were essential for this job, as was a good pair of comfortable shoes as one was on one's feet for long

periods. One also had to get used to people not telling the truth but instead giving the answer they thought was the one the researcher wanted to hear or they thought would show themselves in the best light, for example that they used an expensive brand of cooking fat rather than good old-fashioned lard.

Other moneymaking jobs that were mentioned included gardening and babysitting. For the keen gardener who perhaps lived in a flat or a house with a very small garden, this was ideal and there were elderly people who were only too pleased to have a nice kind young woman come to weed the garden that was now too big for them. It was not particularly well paid but there were perks to be had if the house owners had been in the habit of growing vegetables in the past. With their permission she could reinstate the vegetable plot and grow enough to feed them and her family too. As for the baby-sitting, well that was really the job for the student rather than a mother who had been with her own children all day.

Casual evening babysitting was one thing, but a job that was much in demand was that of childminder. One stay-at-home mother wrote: 'Nursery places were scarce and restricted to the disadvantaged, or if the mothers were in demand, to the children of teachers and nurses.' That being the case, the woman who did not fit into either category but needed to return to work, would very often turn to a friend or neighbour with young children to take care of her child during the day. In the Sixties this was very much an informal arrangement.

My son was born in 1965 and it was just after that that I looked after D. There was nothing formal about it. His Mum lived in our road and wished to return to work in London, so I had him from early morning, brought to me in his pyjamas, and taken home bathed and ready for bed, when she returned in the evening. He was six months older than my son but more behind, so they were more like twins and learned everything together, sitting up, talking, walking, potty training, everything really until he was two and a half when his Mum had another baby. I still had him when my second son was born in 1967. The saddest thing was his Mum missing all his firsts, and me having to tell her what he could do and not to say 'gee gee' as he had been told it was a horse! His Dad came home first from work and when he was older D saw him from the window, and was confused because he had two mummies and two daddies and two homes. Like my son D called me Mummy. I told his Dad he must come and fetch him when he got home or sneak in another way so he couldn't be seen. As it was, he was in his cot yelling within fifteen minutes of his mother collecting him.

While a number of women returned to work once their children were at school, some managed to find work where they could have their babies with them. D.R.'s first child was just ready for school when she gave birth to her second daughter in 1963. In the following year, she and her sister took the brave step of opening a craft shop and baby came too. D.R. remarked: 'In the 1950s you were expected to be a stay-at-home wife, by the Sixties women certainly appeared to be more liberated.' She was one of the lucky ones, 'my husband was very fair and we shared everything and there was no inequality in our lifestyle'. She was also one of those who learnt to drive, using the car for school runs and for business, often attending trade fairs in Blackpool, Harrogate and the Lake District.

A number of couples faced a different type of financial pressure, which caused them to delay having children. The husband discovered that if he was to progress in his chosen profession then he needed further training. This would entail more than just going to night school after a day's work; he would be expected to attend full-time either at a university, college of further education or polytechnic in order to gain the required qualifications. This might mean his having either to travel some distance daily or take digs in another town. Much heart-searching went on as they weighed the pros and cons of making a decision. If he stayed as he was, then his chances of promotion and a higher salary were limited, whereas with the additional knowledge and skills he was assured of advancement. Sometimes it was a question of a complete change of direction when a young man realised that the office job he had jumped at on leaving school no longer gave him satisfaction – or a salary on which to support a family. S.T.'s husband decided he wanted to teach, so for the years he was at teacher training college she continued with her life as a district nurse and supported them both. She was not alone, others supported and encouraged their husbands, though it has to be said that the woman needed to be in a reasonably well-paid job to be able to do so.

Towards the end of the decade, financial pressures were just as bad, if not worse. P.T. had continued with her job at the University in Leeds after her marriage in 1965 but when her husband was appointed to a new post in 1967 they moved to a small village in Bedfordshire where they bought a two-year-old three-bedroomed semi-detached house for £3,900. P.T. was able to find work in Stevenage which no doubt assisted the family finances. However a year later her first child was born. 'Money was quite tight at that time on one salary with a mortgage, which wasn't helped when the mortgage rate was raised considerably. However, I consider myself very fortunate in that women were not expected to go straight back to work in those days and leave their children for others to look after. Five years at home with my children, watching them develop from day to day, were very important to us.'

House prices rose rapidly during the 1960s. Then, as now, it is difficult to give meaningful price comparisons, as they depended very much on demand and area – to quote a well-known TV programme it was always very much a question of 'Location, Location, Location'. For example, a three-bedroomed semi in a village in north Norfolk in the early Sixties was bought for £500. For that the buyer got neither a mains water supply nor sewerage disposal; instead there was a well in the garden and an outside toilet; while inside were very basic electrics, consisting of five light sockets, a fifteen-amp socket for an electric cooker and one five-amp socket to take the kettle or the iron or the wireless, or anything else which needed a power point. However, a mortgage of £1,000 enabled a bathroom with a flush toilet to be installed and a cesspit dug in the garden. In 1960, up in what is now Cumbria, Dr A., who had shared a home with her widowed mother, had to find £2,000 to buy a newly built two-bedroomed semi-detached bungalow, when her mother remarried. On the east coast, at Clacton in 1966 a one-off three-bedroomed detached house was purchased direct from the builder for £3,500. In 1968 a three-bedroomed semi in a village near Leicester sold for £3,800 while a year later a cottage needing renovation cost £3,200. Another fact that emerges clearly is that most people were buying semi-detached homes, not necessarily from choice but because they were being built in greater numbers and therefore were more affordable. However, as P.T. pointed out earlier, those who had a mortgage had to contend with fluctuations in the interest rate they had to pay. During the 1960s it rose to a general 6 per cent leaving householders having to find the increase in their repayments from a salary that was not rising at the same rate.

Although not specifically mentioned by contributors, one very popular way to help pay the mortgage was to offer the spare bedroom as a bedsitter to a single lodger. In most three-bedroomed houses, the third, small bedroom was the baby's room, this left the second bedroom, usually at the back of the house and overlooking the garden empty except for the occasional visitor.

In most towns and cities there were independent women, and men too, who needed accommodation, sometimes on a Monday-to-Friday basis. Others, like unmarried women teachers, needed somewhere to live in term-time. Usually, they were little bother, preparing their meals on a gas ring in their room and requiring from the landlady only a change of bedding weekly. For many, the lodger became a family friend and in return for a chance to watch the occasional Sunday night programme on the host family's television, would offer a free babysitting service. For the hosts, more exciting lodgers came in the form of 'theatricals', the actors who were appearing for a month at a time in the town's local repertory theatre. Many of today's old-established actors started their careers like this and families throughout the country can boast that in the 1960s they had 'So-and-So off the telly', living in their home. But whoever they were, lodgers were very good for mortgages!

However, the woman who, for whatever reason, was unable to rent out a room or do any of the suggested ideas, still needed to find even more ways to save money. Cutting down on visits to the hairdresser, making or remodelling her clothes and those of the children had already been exploited. What was left to be exploited? One new home-owning couple furnished entirely on second-hand and donated gifts, except for the bed, which was the cheapest they could buy. In the evening as they sat on two odd dining-room chairs, they listened to a portable radio while they made a hearthrug from rags. A visit to a local jumble sale had provided the material, a bundle of assorted unwearable cotton garments, for a few shillings, while a kind greengrocer had let them have an old potato sack to provide the backing. Neither of them had ever attempted such a project, but a magazine had given them the basic instructions they needed. They enjoyed the fact that they were doing something together. C. said that the rug held a special place in their hearts and when later it was no longer needed, they were reluctant to let it go. But that was not the limit of C.'s 'do-it-themselves'. She turned next to lampshades to cover the naked bulbs lighting each room.

At school, I'd never been much good at art, as my Art mistress constantly told me, but I did enjoy using my hands and I remembered that in the first year at secondary school we had made a basket using wicker and also we'd made decorative mats using raffia. I discovered a little craft shop in town and found that it was now possible to get coloured raffia – we'd only used the natural stuff as school – and I discovered too that they had some interesting shaped lampshade frames. These were quite cheap compared with a shop-bought shade, so home I went with a lantern shaped frame, some skeins of white raffia plus a tube of glue to stick down the ends – and presto, I taught myself how to make a presentable lampshade. Eventually every room in the house had a raffia covered globe or a lantern shape.

C. was not the only one making her own lampshades, for a time it became almost a craze, spurred on by the helpful hints in women's magazines and others. Long before charity shops dominated our high streets, there were lots of little second-hand shops tucked away in areas where they could use the pavement in front of the shop to display some of their wares. Most of these shops were run by small firms, which specialised in house clearances, often for executors of a property who did not wish to undertake the task for themselves. These shops were a happy hunting ground for those setting up home for there you could buy almost anything you could think of. Of course most of the items were 'old-fashioned', coming from houses that had originally been furnished in the Twenties and Thirties and so were cheap to buy; and for the couple who could visualise what could be done with a lick of paint and the changing of a few handles they were an absolute bargain. But there were other treasures to be found among the dusty, musty interiors of these shops, not least good quality linen, tablecloths and napkins, and lampshades, particular those for the central pendant light and the standard lamp. Once the faded material had been removed, then the 'crafty' woman could recover the framework, perhaps using remnants from the curtains she had made for the living room stuck on to a buckram backing to give them the required stiffness. Parchment was also suggested as an ideal material for a lampshade as it gave the maker a chance to paint her own design upon it. This particular fashion sometimes led to people raiding old framed maps and ancient books for suitable items.

When interior designers of the time decreed that lighting should not be limited to one overhead light and possibly a standard lamp, the 'in' thing was to have table lamps discreetly dotted about the room. Thus came the next moneysaving idea, finding suitable bases to go with all the lampshades. By this time, the upwardly-mobile set were drinking wine and since restaurants had been using wine bottles to hold candles on the tables, the obvious answer was to use wine bottles at home as the base for electric lamps. The most decorative bottle was the one containing Mateus rosé, reputed to be the wine most favoured by women. It was an unusual squat, flattened round shape that made it ideal for lamps and presumably the glass in the base was strong enough to take the layman's attempt at boring the hole through which the electrical wire from the light holder suspended in the top of bottle would pass. Experiments were also made with other shaped bottles; the slim lines of the Blue Nun bottle, the brilliant blue of a Bristol Cream sherry and the stark shape of the Black Tower bottle, all were deemed to add a touch of elegance to a 1960s living room.

Less elegant perhaps but eminently practical were the lamp bases made from recycled washing-up liquid bottles. This sounds very *Blue Peter* inspired, but E. who mentioned making these insists that she did not have a television set at the time, so it is possible that her inspiration came from one of the magazines. Take one empty washing-up liquid bottle and cut off the lid part. Next cover the bottle with a piece of vinyl [*Blue Peter*'s 'sticky-backed plastic']: E. used a wood grain effect. Bore a small hole about a half an inch from the bottom. Thread the electric lead out through the hole, finally, fill the container with gravel or dried peas or beans. Connect the wire to the lamp fitment securely and add a shade. E. gave one of these creations to her mother-in-law as a Christmas present in 1965 and it was still in use thirty years later! The following summer two of E.'s close friends got married in different parts of the country. Although invited to the weddings, she and her husband could not afford to make the long journeys which would have also involved overnight expenses, neither had she the spare cash for expensive wedding presents, so she opted for homemade presents. In her local market she found off-cuts of linen in two different colours for just less than £2. From these she was able to make two sets of four place mats with matching table napkins. She already possessed a quantity of embroidery silks so she used these to embellish each mat and napkin. Carefully ironed and pinned to a piece of card, then covered over with some cellophane, the gift looked as if it had come from a craft shop. Yes, it had cost her time and beside other more splendid gifts may have looked insignificant but each of her friends appreciated the love that had gone into the making and more important, they both used these gifts every day.

There must have been countless similar stories throughout the 1960s, but let us refer to a letter that appeared in *Family Circle* magazine. The writer is commenting on a previous letter in which a reader had lamented that she just did not know where the money she had saved by cutting down or doing things herself had gone. Her canny reply was that when she wished to buy something, she first visited the shops to price it up. Then she bought the materials needed to make it, whether it be a garment, cakes or some other item. She then deducted the price of the materials from the cost of the bought item and put the difference into a savings pot, keeping a careful note of how much went in. In due course she was able to raid the pot to treat herself to a trip to the hairdresser, a new lipstick or even treat her husband to an evening at the cinema. One has to admire the resolve of the writer and her strong will. Some of us would have dipped into that pot when an emergency came along, but then, the 1960s women were indeed made of sterner stuff. What they were as homemakers can, perhaps best be summed up in the words of the daughters of a recently-deceased contributor: a graduate mathematician from the University of St Andrews, and Oxford, who had followed a satisfying and useful career before marriage.

Having grown up in the difficult war years, M.P. was a keen 'make-do-and mender' and recycler. She knitted and sewed clothes for her family and ensured the often abundant garden produce never went to waste. This involved everything from making apple juice from windfalls to every year turning blackberries into what her grandson declared to be 'the best bramble jelly ever'. She was a generous soul and a great inspiration.

Chapter Eleven

Uprooted

T hroughout recorded history women have had to adjust to the way of life chosen by their husbands, wherever or whatever that might entail. One cannot help admiring those women who, to escape religious prejudice and persecution in the sixteenth century, crossed the Atlantic in frighteningly small ships to begin a new life in the unknown territory of the east coast of America. Or their later sisters who packed their family belongings into a wagon and set off across that vast country to try to forge a living from agriculture in what at times must have seemed a hostile and barren land. We should spare a thought too, for those who, as the British Empire expanded, accompanied their menfolk to India and Africa and later to Australia and New Zealand. Whether they were the wives of government officials, traders or soldiers, they all had to contend with the vagaries of climates to which they were unused and all that entailed; the deaths of their children – or long-time parting from them if they were sent back to England – and the problems of adjusting to the language and customs of their new environment. Others, particularly the wives of the nineteenth-century missionaries, found themselves in countries as far afield as China having to act as teacher or nurse, a role for which few had been trained. Yet, the majority of these women accepted their lot and got on with it, mainly because as married women it was their duty and if the bond between husband and wife was strong, then it was unthinkable a wife would question the decision to leave home and security and go off to a strange place.

Even by the 1960s, there were very few women who had the means to resist when their husband suddenly announced that the new job he had applied for was not down the road or even in a different town but – abroad! It was in December 1959 that G.'s father dropped the bombshell that he had been offered work in Australia. When talking it over with his wife, painting a rosy picture of the life that could be theirs, getting away from the overcrowding at home, a bigger wage that would allow them to enjoy a better way of life than they would ever have in Britain, the opportunities for the children, the fresh air and wide open spaces – as the list went on, it was the mention of days of endless sunshine that clinched it for her. She was at that time suffering from severe chilblains, which afflicted her every winter, and the thought of getting away from all that a British winter entailed was a glorious prospect. On the downside, they had to consider that with Australia being on the other side of the world taking their decision to go would mean they might never see their parents and siblings again. In 1960 the possibility of being able to afford to hop on a plane and make a visit home was not a realistic option. Probably neither one of the couple had realised that G.'s father would be flown out by the company to whom he was contracted, leaving her mother not only to do all the packing up but also the selling of the house and furniture. That done, she then had to face the long sea voyage coping with the two children, the eldest aged seven and G. who was just two. Apparently the rocking motion of the ship upset the little girl so much that she refused to walk the whole time she was on board. The good ship *Fairsea* certainly didn't live up to its name and most of the passengers, including our little family, were seasick, not only during the bad weather in the English Channel but also throughout most of the long voyage. Meals on board were served at different times for the children and adults, so G.'s mother had to leave the children alone in the cabin while she tried to eat a hasty meal. She was already thin but by the time she arrived in Australia it was said she looked like a survivor from a refugee camp.

The 1960s saw the start of what became known as 'the Brain Drain'. The clever young men who had gone from grammar school to university in the Fifties and had found employment in one of the burgeoning new industries like computer science, specialised engineering such as aeronautics or nuclear physics, were not only ambitious but were highly sought after. In 1963, M.'s husband was working for the Atomic Energy Authority. In the seven years of their marriage, after two job changes, they were then living in their third house, having started off renting two rooms in an old lady's home before buying their first house. Now mother of three, M., a qualified teacher, had settled to the life of a housewife. Activities outside the home centred mainly on their local church which also gave her the opportunity to entertain members of the congregation at home to Sunday tea, or to coffee after the evening service when they gathered for a discussion.

In August 1963, following the longest, coldest, snowiest winter for decades, M.'s husband applied for a post with a company in Princeton, New Jersey, USA and got it. At which point everything must have seemed slightly surreal. M. recalled:

We all had to apply for permission to live in the US – a Green card called Resident Alien. We went very early by car to London, the children still in their pyjamas until they woke properly and dressed. We parked near the US Embassy in Grosvenor Square. Once inside the Embassy it was a truly gruelling experience for all of us Brits who were waiting to be seen. Staff treated us with scorn; we were rushed round for questioning and given a medical examination by a very gruff doctor. The nicest person was the Consul himself. We had to swear that we would be entering the US for legal reasons and not prostitution! That was me and our three-year-old daughter! After all that we discovered we had insufficient paperwork so we then had to go to Somerset House and search through enormous books to get full birth certificates which were sent by post later. [M and her husband had been born in the 1930s when it was common practice for registrars to issue only a very shortened form of a birth certificate. In some cases, a child would not be named but merely registered as 'boy' or 'girl'.]

When it came to moving we had to sell a lot, including the Broadwood piano that went for £5.0.0 and was trundled away down the road on a trolley; the three piece suite, carpet, heater, pots and pans etc all went. We kept the Ercol dining furniture (we still have it; it having crossed the Atlantic twice, the North Sea and been in ten different houses!), beds, boys' bunks and books and other favourite things plus the car. A removal van from Southampton came and took everything away, not completely packed, so some things never got to us ... Several days later we boarded the SS *United States*. The cabin had two sets of bunks beds so the youngest boy and the girl had to sleep 'top to tail'. It was all very basic – no toilet. But at least we did have a porthole. We had to use handrails in the corridors to get to the bathrooms. The children and I were all seasick. But one day we did manage to get to the swimming pool which was at the bottom of the boat. One of the children thought it was a big hole! The water was choppy but the lifeguard strapped a 'peanut' made of cork around their waists and they happily bobbed about. We reached New York four and a half long days later and had to go through immigration. This took place in the First Class Lounge – what a difference! No more Ellis Island.

They were met by one of her husband's future colleagues who drove them the fifty miles or so south to Princeton where they stayed in a motel for two weeks. Motels were only just making their appearance close to trunk roads in the UK. It seemed to M. that this motel was situated in the busiest place on earth. 'Lorries had lights around the framework so you could see how high and wide they were. [Juggernauts were a rarity on our roads in the early 1960s.] We were taken to a supermarket to buy basic supplies as the motel room had a little kitchen so I could cook. The supermarket was huge and many items were strange.'

Having just come from a market town in the south of England with a small Woolworth's and even smaller M&S, the closest that it came to having a supermarket was the International Stores which was just going over to self-service, otherwise it was still full of individual shops; the butcher, baker, fishmonger, greengrocer and so on as well everything else one could need. Although Britain had passed through the post-war restrictions of the 1950s and imported goods were in greater supply, the US was years ahead in such things as refrigeration and frozen foods as well as unrestricted supplies of meat and home-produced vegetables and fruit unavailable in this country.

M. found the people of Princeton were very welcoming, seemingly always smiling, especially at the sight of the three little Brits dressed in their best M&S tweed coats that were so fashionable in the UK at that time. Once the family had settled into a rented bungalow, she took the children to a large department store to buy winter outfits for them so they would fit in with the other children at school. Although in her account she does not say so, it is obvious that the whole process of settling-in was left to her. Naturally her husband, the breadwinner, would be at work, so it was up to her, as was the norm, to attend to such things as buying clothes, finding a school for the older child, a part-time kindergarten for the second boy and a nursery place three days a week for the little girl. Another surprise in store for her was learning to cook American style.

Scales were not used only measuring jugs (cups) and spoons. We had a large fridge/freezer, huge washing machine and dryer and a dishwasher. Since the house was built on the side of a hill the back opened on to the patio, but to go to the front door we went up six steps and then up another six to the main living area. The weather was cold in winter with snow, but no wind or humidity. Spring was very short and summer long and hot. Autumn was wonderful. We had never seen such trees.

Again the family found a spiritual home in the local Baptist church where they were made most welcome and offered practical advice on schools, where to shop and so on. M. found this support very reassuring, as she was very homesick at first. Three years later they were on the move again. This time it was to Houston in Texas, not only an entirely different part of that vast country, but also a very different way of life from that of Princeton. Her husband had joined the exciting world of space exploration working at NASA.

For a picture of what life was like in Houston we turn to P., whose husband was another ex-pat 'brain' who went to work for NASA.

Houston was a bit of a shock. First the humidity is just like walking into a steam-filled room, the sun is very bright and when it does rain it is a bit like standing under a hose. It is very flat but it was greener than I was expecting. On my first visit to a supermarket I discovered that everything really is bigger in Texas … milk and ice cream came in gallon containers, crisps came in large drums and there was a taste difference to a lot of things. [In 1960s Britain milk still came in one-pint glass bottles, generally delivered to your doorstep in the early morning by either a local dairy or one of the large companies such as the Co-op or Express Dairies. Ice cream was normally sold in single portions or perhaps in small blocks. As for crisps, these still came only in small bags.] Everywhere was air-conditioned.

We were renting an apartment which had a large living room and a kitchen/dining area at one end, two bedrooms and a bathroom. The apartment complex also had a laundrette and pool. We quickly became friends with our neighbours across the landing. They had only moved in a month before us and were from Pennsylvania so we got to do a lot of things together. We found people were very friendly and out-going. Mostly they had moved into the area too, as Houston was a rapidly expanding city and the American 'can do' approach to everything was everywhere.

After the birth of our daughter in 1965 [her son was then almost two] we decided we needed more room and bought a house in a new development … This was a 'ranch-style' bungalow with three bedrooms, a large open plan den, dining area and kitchen, two bathrooms, a smaller living-room and a double garage. There was a primary school newly built and some small shops. Later a supermarket was added and it was not far from a small mall and other facilities. We enjoyed the outdoorsy lifestyle of picnics and barbecues.

To a young woman coming from England this must have seemed like entering a dream world. What a contrast the ranch-style bungalow with its two bathrooms and open-plan living was to the type of three-bedroom semis which were going up on estates all over Britain at that time, many without garages, never mind a double one. However, there was a downside to this 'glamorous' life.

First there was the heat. By August and September you longed for a cool breeze. Mosquitoes were a problem. Plus you had to spray your house to keep out large cockroaches. Not dangerous, but not nice. At the time we lived there Houston had a very high murder rate so most people owned a firearm of some sort. When I had my son in England I had a very easy home delivery with midwife, her junior and my husband attending. Our GP made it just as everything was over. However giving birth in the US was very depressing. I <u>had</u> to go to hospital. I <u>had</u> to have a full anaesthetic and 'NO' my husband could not be present. Think of the germs! I even got the feeling that breast-feeding did not really meet their approval because one couldn't monitor exactly how much the baby was getting.

In many ways the women who either emigrated or lived in another country for any length of time were much more likely to integrate into the way of life in the host country than their husbands. This was particularly so for those who had young children who would soon be starting school. It was essential that mother should be able to participate in related activities and of course, for her it was a way of making friends and acquaintances. It was easier if the host country was English-speaking but if it was not, then the woman needed to pick up as much as she could of the language in order to be able not only to shop but also to communicate with school, the doctor, the bus driver … the list goes on. Often it was the case that when in a foreign country, the husband would spend his working day amongst English speakers and yet remain unable to communicate with the local population. But it wasn't only in areas where English was a second language that English women could find themselves not being able to converse with those around them. When B. had her whirlwind courtship in 1963 with the handsome American airman she met in the newly-opened bowling alley of her hometown she was just nineteen. They met in March and by the time his unit was sent home to the States in July, she was pregnant. She followed in August to find that her new home was living on a remote farm in Pennsylvania Dutch country with her husband's brother and his family.

> I went from high heels and nail polish to farm attire in one day. We got married in a very simple ceremony. Although I was pregnant I was expected to work hard on the farm. I felt very isolated as they all spoke Pennsylvania Dutch. On Sunday we all went to church. I was stared at, talked about and avoided by the older German people. They had no idea where England was! They had come from Germany as children and started work after the 8th grade in school. I was homesick and could not relate to the women around me. I was so glad when we moved about 120 miles away. Then I was alone with my baby most of the time as my husband worked long hours. In New Jersey most people were Italian so I still didn't fit in. We did get to know some neighbours in the apartment complex but I was always 'that English woman' though and I was never sure who wanted to be a friend. We moved a lot, money was always a concern until 1971 but that's another story.

In some ways there is a similar pattern in A.'s story. Like many 1960s girls, she left her grammar school at sixteen after taking the General Certificate of Education. Her first job was in the records department of her local hospital. Probably, if she had been asked, she would have admitted that music records interested her far more than medical ones. And, again like many others, she was itching for the chance to get away from home and live her own life. Her chance came the following year when at seventeen she met her serviceman boyfriend and promptly fell in love. Within the year she had what was known in the Sixties as a 'shotgun wedding', a quiet affair arranged by her parents who would not have given their permission had she not been pregnant, as she was officially under age. However, the parents saw that she had a proper wedding; she wore a pretty white dress, which did not reveal her condition, and the happy couple honeymooned in Cornwall with very little money.

Their first posting as a couple was to Germany and their living conditions must have been a shock to a girl who had been brought up in a comfortable home. Just as in England there was still a housing shortage, it was much worse in Germany. A. takes up her story:

We lived in two rooms at the top of the house. The only water supply was two floors down and I could never get the nappies dry. It was the winter of 1963, quite awful; my poor son had constant nappy rash. The living room where he slept was heated by a fire but our bedroom was freezing. Our landlady could not resist telling me (in German) how to live my life, care for the baby and live! She used the phrase 'zie mussen – you must' which always brought the unspoken response from me 'no, I must not', We moved later to two much nicer rooms in a farmhouse, with a delightful English-speaking landlady who was probably something between a friend and a second mum to me. We were able to help ourselves to vegetables produced on the farm and could pay for bread, eggs and beer at the end of week. Once we were settled our landlady would baby-sit so that we could visit Jazz cellars for an evening. They were smoky, lively places.

A. admits now that she and her husband were not only very young in actual years, but in many ways they were both still immature. They had hardly had time to get to know each other when the baby arrived and then they had to face up to the responsibilities of parenthood. That at times their relationship was stormy was borne out by their dented saucepans! She did her cooking on a Baby Belling, a tiny electric hotplate with a minute oven below. Her husband worked long hours so she often felt very lonely and isolated. To relieve this, she would find a job for herself and a childminder for her son. She can probably still tell you today the German names for the flowers and plants she sold when working in a florist shop. She also manned the till in the local NAAFI for a time. None of the jobs she took lasted for long though, as she said herself, 'I only stayed for a couple of weeks or months till I felt better or the weather changed'. Certainly a good way to avoid sinking into a deep depression! Towards the end of the Sixties, A.'s husband was a sergeant in charge of a section in Cyprus. There, with the experience and confidence of a 26-year-old, was when, A. says, she started her social work. As the wife of a sergeant and the oldest wife on the base, it often fell to her when the men were away to look after all the very young wives and their babies. Unlike others who may have come into military life later, she really knew and understood the problems they were facing. It was a good time for her too; she had a car, so she had freedom, and the weather was warm and sunny!

The wives of regular servicemen were faced with two alternatives, either they stayed at home while their men were away for long periods, as was often the case for those in the navy, or they led a peripatetic life both in Britain and overseas as their husbands were moved from one base to another. Although these women were usually provided with housing on site, this meant that they had little opportunity to create the home they would have liked for their family. It was often difficult to put down roots in an area that was totally unknown and to make friends beyond the Barracks. For the children there was the upheaval of constant changes of school. Many adults brought up as service children admit to gaps in their academic knowledge as a result of arriving in the middle of a subject on the syllabus, particularly harmful in Maths or Science. Then there was the boredom of doing the Anglo-Saxons three times but missing out on the Civil War or reading a set text more than once. For men deployed abroad in non-combat areas, if their wives accompanied them, then the teenage children were likely to be sent home to boarding school.

As we have already seen, the 1960s saw a great number of British women whose husbands' work had taken them abroad. Commonwealth countries throughout the world had been governed and policed by British men; similarly much of the industry of each country had been financed and run by them too. As prosperity increased then British firms looked to create and maintain a flourishing market for their products. Thus at an ex-pat club in Northern Nigeria, for example, you would find the wives of the men responsible for running the iron mines, maintaining the road links and the railway as well as a brewery representative, the manager of the local department store, the boys' school headmaster and the salesman for window blinds and shutters, as well as the area representative for a medical charity.

For the wives who had come straight out from the UK, where they had either worked or had been a stay-at-home housewife, the change in lifestyle was dramatic. Like Service wives, they found themselves provided with a company house, equipped with standard furnishings, possibly in an ex-pat compound. Unlike the regulation barracks' housing, solid brick terraces, uniform and lacking in character, the ex-pats had spacious, airy bungalows with verandas on all sides or rather imposing mansion-type houses that could have been used on the set for *Gone with the Wind*. Each house would have had a garden with exotic plants including banana trees and sweet smelling bougainvillea. But all this grandeur came at a price that took some getting used to. Quite apart from the heat, one of the first things to become accustomed to was the length of daylight hours. Being close to the equator, daylight came early and darkness fell in early evening. How often have we in Britain wished for long days of sunshine and complained bitterly when instead there has been nothing but cold persistent rain but at least we knew that it was bound to clear up soon and the sun would shine. More difficult to live with endless sunshine, desert winds that cover every inch of the house with dust and a heat that is so intense you long for the day when the monsoon will bring rain. It took time for the ex-pat women's bodies to acclimatise to these conditions, so it was just as well that their lifestyle was so very different to that of home. To a young woman who had lived at home with a mother who did the cooking, cleaning and laundry and a father who took care of the gardening, general maintenance and made sure her shoes were shined for school, it came as a shock when she learned she would now have to manage servants instead. For the average British girl the closest contact she might have had with domestic service would have been with the 'obliging' lady who came for a couple of hours once or twice a week to help with the housework. Now, here she was in a foreign country, totally unlike home, with every aspect of her household taken care of by a number of the local inhabitants, all of whom were men! It took time to accept having her personal washing and ironing dealt with by a man. But she soon found her feet, even though it seemed strange to be giving orders and soon her 'houseboys' were simply part of her extended family.

The biggest problem these women had to face was boredom. There was a limit to the number of coffee mornings or bridge/canasta afternoons one could attend. It helped if one had a hobby that could be pursued either alone or with others. Better still if she could find some form of employment but opportunities for that were very limited. Social life for ex-pats revolved round the Club. There was the swimming pool, the restaurant, the dance hall, the games rooms and so on. Films could be shown outside on the terrace under starlit skies, concerts arranged either by themselves or given by visiting artists. This type of concentrated living meant that social circles tended to become very close. With husbands often away for a week or two on business in remote areas, or husbands temporarily 'single' while their wives went home to the UK to have a baby or see to the needs of elderly parents, there were always sufficient friends and colleagues to rally round and keep the lonely one company. It was here under such circumstances, that affairs, casual or eventually serious enough to lead to divorce, occurred.

Someone who thoroughly enjoyed life living in a hot country with uncertain climatic conditions was C. who in 1964 had married a newly-qualified chartered accountant, earning about £10 a week.

When in 1966 he had the promise of doubling that to £20, it seemed a great adventure to go and live in the Caribbean on a three-year contract.

September saw us setting sail for Jamaica to a new country, a new life and a new six-week-old baby son. Seen off at Southampton by both families we boarded the Italian line ship the *Caribia*. It all seemed very exciting to be sailing on a beautiful ship across the Atlantic to start a new life. I had only ever been to Europe, Spain in particular, on holiday, so life in the Caribbean seemed so far away and very exotic. We had managed to find a book about Jamaica – it only had black and white photos – which we read but that was just about all we knew about the country we were going to.

We had a wonderful time on the ship, stopping at Vigo in Spain and Funchal in Madeira before the long crossing to Kingston. We got to know the hundred or so other passengers –all Europeans – and I danced with the Captain and Officers at the wonderful evening parties. We reached Jamaica at night and sailed down the south coast to Kingston. I could see all these twinkling lights on the land, it looked like fairyland and in the morning when we saw the Island for the first time it was just as Sir Francis Drake had said when he first saw Jamaica –'The most beautiful island the eye had ever seen'. We disembarked next morning and were met by one of the partners [in the firm] and his wife.

I pushed my baby in his brand new pram into a large hangar which was teeming with black people. This was my first big culture shock. They were meeting all their relations off the ship we had been on and we didn't have a clue they were on board. I had only seen a few black people in London and to see so many all at once was quite intimidating, and it made me quickly realise how they must have felt when they first arrived in England. At least we had arrived in beautiful sunshine and had a place to live. They had had pouring rain, fog and were homeless.

The house we rented was a bungalow as most properties were, and although the furnishings were pretty dire (I had left all my lovely Heals furniture behind) the garden was a 'garden of Eden'. There were pineapples, bananas, plantains, sweet and sour sops, as well as lime and orange trees. Most of these fruits I had never tasted.

Jamaican cuisine was my second big revelation. I thought it was wonderful but my husband wasn't nearly so keen. His first job was at a plantation on the north coast, and when lunch was served he had curried goat with green boiled bananas, rice and peas with what he thought was pickled peppers but was actually the hottest, fiery pepper sauce. Having probably only had a 'Vesta' curry before, he said it nearly blew his head off! I loved all the food. We had Jamaican parties at lunchtime washed down with the local Red Stripe beer and sometimes Salt fish and Akee for breakfast, which to this day I still have to cook for my children as a treat.

I didn't drive so I was taken shopping by my new friend Jill. The supermarket wasn't like Sainsbury's and had things I'd never seen before; pickled pigs' tails; very smelly salted mackerel; salt cod; Jack fish and goat. Fruit and vegetables included green oranges; yam, sweet potatoes, calaloo and scallion to name but a few. However the supermarkets always had shortages of basic things and as they exported most of the sugar, we often couldn't find it anywhere!

All the homes had burglar bars at the windows and most had guard dogs in the garden. Security was always an issue as unemployment was very high and there was no unemployment benefit or pension. Most homes employed a maid and a gardener, so with Jill's help I employed a maid called Rose. It was very strange to have another person share our home but she had her own maid's quarters at the back of the house. She did all the housework, washing and ironing and was wonderful with our baby. (I wish I had her now!) We only had one problem with one of her boy friends who pulled a knife on her one night; fortunately my husband was able to reason with him until he went away.

I didn't get too homesick but I really looked forward to writing to family and receiving letters from home. Phone calls were very expensive and had to be booked in advance and then went through the operator and then the cable under the sea, often the echo on the line was terrible. I filled my days with reading when not meeting friends. Social life was wonderful, lots of parties, dinner parties, dining out, cards, tennis, squash and badminton and of course going to the beach. We made friends from all nationalities, Jamaican, Lebanese, Syrian, Chinese, Indian, American and of course, ex-pats.

The weather was mostly wonderful but we did have a rainy season when the heavens would open and it would pour down for a couple of hours and then the sun would come out and everything would steam. We were always ready for the hurricane season. We had a special hurricane store cupboard for food, candles etc. and the bath had to be filled with water. Everything outside that was loose had to be secured and windows boarded up but we were very lucky and never had one come on land during the time we were there although they came very close several times.

At the end of three years, C.'s husband was offered a partnership in the firm, so after a holiday back home, they returned for another seven years. When asked if she could contribute her experiences, her initial response was that she didn't know if she could remember enough or express it adequately. What you have just read is only an extract but the details recorded as seen through the eyes of a young woman in her twenties, have certainly added another dimension to the picture of life in the 1960s. Incidentally, C. thoroughly enjoyed writing her memoirs!

While C. can recall with great detail much of the time she spent in the Caribbean and her abiding love of the country, yet with much the same time lapse since those events, P.M.'s recollections are very different. She had led a very sheltered life, having left school at fifteen and gone to work locally in the darkroom of the Ilford Film Developing plant. She was never, by her account, either a giddy schoolgirl or a teenager immersed in popular music and the latest fashions. Her life revolved around her home and family. She met her future husband when she was eighteen at her sister's wedding. They started going out, got engaged when she was twenty-one and planned to marry in March 1963. It was in the months leading up to the wedding that her fiancé broke the news that he intended to give up working on a farm and that once they were married they would be emigrating to New Zealand. After all this time P.M. has little recollection of what preparations were needed for this bold step in the way of interviews, medicals and so forth; one suspects that she had been brought up to believe that all such details should be left to the man. Her recollection now is that at the time she greeted the whole thing as a great adventure. So there they were, three weeks after their wedding on a Quantas charter flight with other emigrants, most likely all of them on the government assisted passage scheme, flying via the USA and landing in Australia from where they took a further flight, to New Zealand. Not bad going for a girl who had never flown before or even left British soil for a holiday. P.M. did recall that as they flew over New Zealand she had looked down through the window and was struck by the thought 'I don't know a living soul in this country'. It was Easter when they arrived. Their heavy luggage and her husband's Norton Dominator motorcycle had been sent ahead by sea, so once they had reclaimed that, they were able to set off travelling. They ended up in the Upper Hutt valley on North Island where they lodged with an elderly lady. P.M. helped look after the lady, while her husband went off and found work – not on a farm, as one might have expected but in Dunlop's tyre factory. Work was not only plentiful in those days, it was also well paid. So it was not long before they could afford to put down a deposit on a bungalow, far larger than anything they could have had in England. P.M. settled to making a home for them and she even found time to get a job. They did not have a wide social circle as most of the people around them were much older, and in any case, as P.M. said, they were not the party-going types. Gone now are details of such things as food, shopping and leisure pursuits. Asked how she felt at that time, she said she had settled, although it took time to be accustomed to the occasional earthquake. She related how one evening when her husband was on late shift, she heard for the first time what sounded like a very heavy lorry coming down the street. She looked out of the window but there was no vehicle in sight: the rumbling was that of an earth tremor. Just over a year after her wedding, in 1964 P.M. gave birth to her daughter. Again she did not volunteer any information about whether the birth was in hospital or at home. But it was having the baby that totally unsettled her, awakening the overwhelming desire to go home to see her family. A holiday back in the UK was beyond their means and so she bore the acute homesickness the best she could. Fortunately she had by this time acquired a woman friend who, in many ways became a mother substitute to her but also encouraged P.M. in her religious faith. As far as P.M. is concerned this was the most important thing that occurred during her time in New Zealand. Another daughter arrived in August 1966 and then P.M. finally got her way and in January 1967 the family boarded the Italian ship *Fair Star* for the long voyage back home. Tentatively asking the question did she regret coming back, she thought that, had she been able to come home for a holiday, she would have gone back and been more settled. But then hindsight is a wonderful thing.

Every so often similarities appear in the lives of contributors. For example A.J., like P.M. and M.O., came from a family which did not encourage much in the way of a social life outside the home. All three left school at fifteen, although both A.J. and M.O. did further their general education while studying for qualifications that took them into secretarial work, while P.M. went into factory work, as did a number of the other contributors. But the strangest similarity came with M.O. and A.J., both of whose future husband was the very much younger brother of their mothers' best friend. A.J.'s mother and her friend arranged a trip, which included A.J. and the brother, on the *Queen of the Channel* steamer from Clacton to Calais. However, severe fog in the Channel meant that they never made it to the French coast on that autumn Sunday in 1961, but at least during the voyage the young people had someone to talk to. It was the summer of 1962 before he contacted her again, by letter, telling her that he had joined the RAF. Courtship followed and they married in February 1964. In the early part of 1965, just as A.J. discovered she was pregnant, her husband was put on a preliminary warning for overseas service, but he was allowed to apply for deferment until the baby was born. At that time, most postings were to Germany, Cyprus or the Far East, but they were told they would be going to Nairobi in Kenya.

A.J. takes up the story:

In my teens I'd read a book about game parks in Africa, where you could drive along a road with wild animals grazing nearby and thought 'how fantastic', never, ever thinking I'd be able to visit Africa … We landed at 9am on 8 November and my first impressions were of the wide skies (just like East Anglia) and how bright it was … November was the time of the 'short rains' and there was a short shower that morning followed by all these flying creatures which seemed like huge flies, not mosquitoes as I thought, but harmless termites one soon got used to. We lived in an RAF flat, equipped with all the basics, that had the most magnificent views over the Nairobi golf course to the plains beyond with Mount Kilimanjaro in the distance. Within days of our arrival, Ian Smith declared UDI for Southern Rhodesia and a boycott was imposed on all imports and exports. This left Zambia, which got all its oil and other goods by rail through Southern Rhodesia, isolated. The British government arranged for barrels of oil to be flown into Zambia by the RAF, first from a base in Tanzania but then from Nairobi – my husband was involved because of his RAF trade of air traffic control.

Although some families had a house servant, I didn't, so daily life was much like England. I bought most of my groceries in the NAAFI store. I really missed both Robertson's marmalade and Heinz beans. The latter sometimes appeared in the NAAFI but only in small tins, which cost the equivalent of 5/-. I used the local shops for bread, fruit and vegetables, both plentiful and cheap. Meat was generally cheaper than in England, chickens could be tough but there were very good sausages, bacon and pies from a local bacon factory. Oxo cubes were made locally as was Lux soap. Margarine came in tins, opened with a tin opener, as did a 'box of chocolates', while milk came in one pint cans from a grocery store. There was a Woolworth's in the city centre and a shop, which stocked items from Marks and Spencer's – I bought a handbag there and when I returned home, my sister had one identical!

The local radio had a popular 'Housewife's Choice' programme in the morning and we also listened to the BBC World Service. At Christmas the radio station did a 'Radio for the Blind' charity event where people rang up and pledged money to have a particular record played – the first Christmas we were there the Beatles' 'Yellow Submarine' and 'I was Kaiser Bill's Batman' were popular requests. There was television with just one channel that broadcast only in the evening except on Sundays when it broadcast in the afternoon as well. There were a number of cinemas in the city including two drive-in ones, which were very useful if you had young children.

Among the people calling to sell items, was an elderly African man who sold flowers. He came every Friday morning at the same time with his ancient bicycle – flat tyres, no pedals or chain, but very valuable to him as he used it for support and to hang the baskets of flowers on the handlebars. One day he didn't come until much later, walking slowly with a stick and carrying just a few flowers. He told us his bike had been stolen. He came only a few times after that. An old broken cycle that in England would long ago have been scrapped had had such great value to him, providing him with the means to make a living.

We took every advantage of seeing the sights and scenes offered. We drove down to Mombasa, a journey of around three hundred miles, partly on dirt roads, for a holiday and had a trip out to the coral reef. We also frequently visited the Nairobi game park or the animal orphanage attached to it. Friends introduced us to fishing and once we spent a week at Lake Naivasha. While the men fished we women walked, watching hippos coming out of the lake to graze with the cows. We also went to the snake park where we saw a thirty-foot-long python and lots of poisonous snakes kept in a concrete pit that were 'milked' to provide an antidote to snake bites. Then there were all the magnificent trees in the arboretum; jacarandas with their beautiful blue flowers lined the city centre streets. I discovered many wild flowers growing on the edge of the golf course, 'Gloriosa Lilies' which climbed up through the trees, Acidethera which is a highly scented white gladioli, Star of Bethlehem plants and a very tiny 'African Violet' like flower which appeared in the grass overnight once the rains started.

A.J. returned with her family to England in June 1967. The two years spent in Africa had opened her eyes to experiences shared with only a few of us. Unlike P.M., she embraced the opportunity she had been given and although it was but a short time out of her life it has remained etched vividly in her memory.

For many of the women transplanted to countries where it was taken for granted that they would have servants to cater for their every need, the prospect proved daunting although it did not take them long to accept it. Let us spare a thought for those who like R.H. was brought by her British husband to live in England in the early 1960s. R.H. was a well-educated young woman, brought up in an affluent Anglo-Malaysian home. When she married her expatriate husband she anticipated that her domestic life would mirror that of her mother. And so it did until Malaya gained independence from Britain and her husband's position changed, leading him to decide it was time for him to return to England. On arrival the couple and their two small children stayed with R.H.'s in-laws in Surrey. And it was here she had her first shock following the 'welcome home' meal. Not only was there no servant to clear away the dishes, there was no one to wash them either. The women of the family performed this task. R.H. was astonished, to say the least. But worse was in store when she and her husband managed to find a house of their own into which they moved during the worst winter possible, that of 1963. The only heating in the house came from the coal fire in the sitting room. R.H.'s husband showed her how to lay the fire with paper and sticks and then small coals. All of this was totally alien to her. Her initial attempt to follow her husband's trick to get the fire to draw by holding a sheet of newspaper in front of it resulted in the paper catching alight before eventually flying up the chimney. Then she, who had never done so before, was confronted with doing the family laundry. The washing, she knew, had to be hung on the washing line but when she came to take it in, she could not understand why each garment was hanging stiffly. R.H. can laugh about it now but the culture shock she suffered at the time was greater than anything the previous women had suffered. Quite apart from going from being a lady of leisure to a normal British housewife, she had to withstand the looks and comments of the curious for mixed-race couples were rare in Surrey at that time.

Chapter Twelve

Pure Nostalgia

For the benefit of social historians in the future but mainly to refresh the memories of those who were there, here are some of the musicians, writers, films and plays mentioned by my 1960s women.

The Sixties was my favourite decade for music. I remember Cilla Black, Jim Reeves, Englebert Humperdink, Milly of 'My Boy Lollipop' fame and the Bee Gees, especially Robin Gibb when he broke away to release a single. The Beatles weren't the only group; there were The Seekers, The Batchelors and Abba. In 1967, Sandie Shaw won the Eurovision Song Contest for England, singing 'Puppet on a String', in bare feet. Films included *Alfie*, *The Sound of Music* and *Georgy Girl*, all three of which had favourite pop songs of the time associated with them.

I still remember *The Sound of Music*, *Butch Cassidy and the Sundance Kid*, *Grand Prix*, *Those Magnificent Men in their Flying Machines* and *The Plank*, which is still shown on TV fairly regularly and still funny. A couple of books which left their mark were Han Suyin's *The Mountain is Young* and *A Many Splendoured Thing* and Elspeth Huxley's *Flame Trees of Thika*.

Music – folk and jazz but most of The Beatles. The Rolling Stones were also very popular but they were a bit too wild and scruffy for us. We supported the Mods not the Rockers. Didn't go to the cinema much but we did all go down to a cinema in South London to see *Dr No* – the first James Bond Film. We loved it.

Nat King Cole, Mat Monroe, The Beatles – some jazz – Elvis Presley, Peggy Lee and Cliff Richard. Sometimes went to a 'Carry On' film.

My husband and I were fans of Andy Williams, Val Doonican, Burt Baccarat and Dionne Warwick. We never really got into Rock & Roll.

The group who had a hit when we became engaged (1967) was Procul Harem, with 'A Whiter Shade of Pale'. We loved Bob Dylan, Dave

Brubek, Miles Davis, Nina Simone, The Stones and the Beatles, of course. Other groups which come to mind which we enjoyed were The Hollies, The Dave Clark Five, Sonny and Cher, Herman's Hermits, Manfred Mann and the Motown groups. Films I remember enjoying include *The Graduate*, *Blow Up*, *The Great Escape*, *Saturday Night and Sunday Morning*, *Dr Zhivago*, *The Pink Panther*, *The Birds*, *Tom Jones*, *Goldfinger*, *Butch Cassidy and the Sundance Kid* and *The Longest Day*.

[Note. In the 1960s films did not always go on general release following their debut in London. The large chains, Odeon and ABC, were the first to show what were expected to be major box office draws. The small independent cinemas often had to wait before they could show them which accounts for why people throughout the country saw films at different times of the year – or even the next one.]

My taste in music was pop, especially The Beatles and Cliff Richard. To listen though I often had to resort to tuning in to Radio Luxemburg or the pirate station Radio Caroline under the bed covers

Memorable music has to include The Beatles, The Rolling Stones, Eddie Cochrane, The Everley brothers, and of course, Elvis. During long car journeys my sister and I would sing all the words from every Rodgers and Hammerstein musical by heart. Later I was awarded singing lessons where we sang scales and then pieces like 'Where e'er you Walk' or 'Sweet lass of Richmond Hill'. I was more interested in 'Anyone Who Has a Heart' (Cilla) and 'You've Lost that Loving Feeling' (the Righteous Brothers).

Music – Beatles (saw them live in Southampton around 1962), Rolling Stones, Beach Boys, Buddy Holly, Gene Vincent, Elvis Presley, Little Richard (those were the days!). Went to the cinema quite often – remember *Blow Up* (I think it was called) – trendy black and white film – probably one of the last, *Doctor Zhivago*, *Dr Strangelove*, the Bond films and *The Graduate*.

The music scene was amazing. The Beatles who I still love today were the best ever. Then there were The Beach Boys, The Rolling Stones, The Kinks, The Hollies, Dusty Springfield, who I think is brilliant, The Four Seasons. A group called The Walker Brothers came over from America and I fell in love with Scott Walker. His poster was above my pillow and looked down on me. Then there was Stevie Wonder, Billy Kramer and The Dakotas. They were all fab.

Last Words

In 1967 we had a three-week visit back to England [from the US]. I noticed how very mini the skirts were and had to take my hems up! Business seemed to be booming in the country at that time.

The 1960s for me for me was a very challenging time; looking back I'm amazed I packed in so much.

The fashions at that time were great … Miniskirts, Mary Quant styles in Op Art (black and white.) Twiggy and great hairstyles. We felt as if we were on a different planet from our parents.

We were very lucky to be young in the 1960s. We had the benefits of free tertiary education, excellent employment prospects, no problems with housing, increasing prosperity and choice. We lived in exciting times. Women now had equal opportunities to men and they had a reliable form of contraception which enabled them to plan their lives as never before. The Sixties were indeed swinging. (The word now has a very different meaning but I use the old meaning.)

Looking back it does seem the Swinging Sixties passed me by. Although I was very much aware of all the changes going on I was too much in awe of my parents to be much of a rebel. I had decided on medicine as a career by the time I was 13–14 and I knew I would have to do well at school to get the necessary O and A level grades. Quite a lot was expected of me in terms of helping at home – I recall mowing the lawn when England won the World Cup – so this plus my studying left little time to even consider serious rebelling, let alone carry it out.

I was aware of the feminist movement but as I always thought I had enough independence, I didn't feel the need to burn my bra!

Why isn't moygashel still available? It looked like linen but had none of the disadvantages.

Money was always very tight. I worked in the fields when the children were small picking currants, potatoes and apples. Then I had a variety of evening jobs, so when my husband got home, I went to work. We did this for a number of years until both children were at school and I could work in the daytime.

Mainly I look back on the 1960s as being a carefree period of my life.

Thank you for this trip down memory lane. I've really enjoyed it.

Life seems to have been simpler back then. I think I missed out on the 'Swinging Sixties' bit somewhere – despite living in London. We knew Christine Keeler lived in the street behind our flat near Baker Street, and after we had moved the Balcombe Street Siege took place a few doors away. Whilst we were there the Beatles were filming at Marylebone Station, just down the road and we went to watch. The station was disguised to look like Liverpool and there were lots of tiny girls screaming and chasing the Beatles into a phone box. That is about the most exciting thing I can remember about that time – sad isn't it?

The Sixties for me were exciting and fulfilling and brought rewards of friendship and ideas I still hold dear today.

I don't think I can contribute much. I was rather involved with three small boys under six. Most world-shattering events seemed to pass me by.

As for the 'Swinging Sixties' we had better things to do and I suspect they passed most of us who were studying and working in nursing etc., unnoticed.

Swinging Sixties? Not really in my life but we didn't live in or around London. Suspect the newspapers and media then were as now London-centred and as far as I'm concerned the whole thing was just a media construct.

I have never been sure what is meant by the Swinging Sixties – I was probably too busy with small children to notice.

I only read about the Swinging Sixties in the newspapers.

Thinking back to how it was for friends and cousins in the Fifties, I think that in the 1960s we had more freedom – in fact everything, the music, fashion and trends was geared to the teenager. We pushed the boundaries. You could go from one job to another when you got fed up with the one you were doing and could get experience in all sorts of careers.

It [answering the questionnaire] has been very thought-provoking, raising many issues. Thanks.

At that time, the young invented the world, as the flappers did in the Twenties. Youth was in ascendancy. Where are all the young trail-blazers now? Watching television or tweeting? They certainly are not changing the world.

Index